Instructor's Manual and Test Bank

for

Women, Men, and Society

Instructor's Manual and Test Bank

for

Renzetti and Curran

Women, Men, and Society
Third Edition

Claire M. Renzetti
Daniel J. Curran
Raquel Kennedy Bergen
St. Joseph's University

ALLYN AND BACON
Boston · London · Toronto · Sydney · Tokyo · Singapore

ISBN 0-205-16679-2

Printed in the United States of America

10 9 8 7 6 5 4 3 2 1   99 98 97 96 95 94

TABLE OF CONTENTS

Introduction

A Note About Films and Videos for Classroom Use

INTRODUCTION

This manual is designed as a resource of methods for evaluating students' understanding of the text material and for stimulating learning through assignments and classroom discussion. The manual, which is also available on disk, includes a test bank composed of multiple-choice, true/false, and essay questions, Classroom activities/take-home assignments and film suggestions also are included. In addition, for most chapters we provide names, addresses and telephone numbers of organizations from which both instructors and students may obtain additional information on specific issues on topics. For some chapters, information also is provided on how to subscribe to various electronic forums.

One of our goals here is to encourage students to draw on their personal gendered experiences and to apply what they have read in the text to their own lives. Some of the suggested exercises also require students to "learn by doing." In this way, we hope to provide students with creative learning experiences and simultaneously help them hone their communication skills, both verbal and written. Instructors may see the exercises as opportunities to enrich their classes by breaking out of a standard lecturing style, and they may appreciate additional ways of evaluating their students' comprehension of the course material besides traditional testing.

We would like to take this opportunity to thank our colleagues who reviewed the second edition of WOMEN, MEN, and SOCIETY and the accompanying test bank. They offered many helpful suggestion for improvements. We view teaching as a collaborative enterprise -- one that evolves and improves through the constructive criticism of colleagues and students. Consequently, we encourage both instructors and students to share with us their experiences in using the third edition of the text and this manual, and we welcome suggestions for revisions.

We would also like to thank Joanne Devlin for her help in typing this manual, and David Lees, director of the Instructional Media Center at St. Joseph's University for compiling and largely writing the note on films and videos for classroom use. A special thank you as well to Julie McDonald, Assistant Professor of Philosophy at St. Joseph's University for her help in identifying relevant electronic forums. The work of Joan Korenman must also be acknowledged. Joan Korenman compiled a list of gender-related electronic forums from the WMST-L file collection (an academic list that focuses on women's studies teaching, research and program administration, but also provides announcements of job openings and conferences, calls for papers, and includes files of syllabi and bibliographies). The list compiled by Joan and passed on to us through Julie was invaluable in the preparation of this manual.

A NOTE ABOUT FILMS AND VIDEOTAPES FOR CLASSROOM USE

The film suggestions in this manual reflect the professional judgment and personal biases of the authors. We think that these materials offer excellent illustrations of many of the specific issues raised in the text; some instructors may not agree and may wish to locate other audio-visual materials more to their own liking. There are a number of comprehensive reference guides to educational films and videos that they might find helpful in this pursuit:

1. FILM AND VIDEO FINDER (3 volumes, 3rd edition, 1991, National Information Center for Education Media [NICEM]; available from Access Innovations, Inc., P.O. Box 40130, Albuquerque, NM 87196): This is an alphabetical listing by title of numerous films and videos on a wide variety of topics. It provides a brief description of each film or video, its running time, and the producer or distributor from whom it is available. NICEM indexes are also available on-line through Dialog Information Services File 46 and on CDROM compact disk. Printed updates are provided.

2. EDUCATIONAL FILM AND VIDEO LOCATOR OF THE CONSORTIUM OF UNIVERSITY FILM CENTERS (2 volumes, 4th edition, 1990-91; available from R.R. Bowker Co., 205 East 42nd Street, New York, NY 10017): This is a compilation of the film/video titles available for rent from the forty-six member universities of the Consortium of University Film Centers. Rental sources follow each descriptive entry. (It is typically less expensive to rent films and videos from a university than from a commercial distributor.)

3. THE VIDEO SOURCEBOOK (2 volumes, 13th edition, 1992, National Video Clearinghouse, Inc.; available from Gale Research Co., Book Tower, Detroit, MI 48226): This guide is published annually and provides descriptions of videotapes available on various topics. However, it gives no rental information other than the producer/distributor.

4. FILMMAKERS LIBRARY CATALOG (124 East 40th Street, New York, NY 10016): Many of the films and videos we suggest come from the Filmmakers Library, an excellent source of audio-visual material for sociology and the other social sciences. Filmmakers Library often has programs that were aired on the Public Broadcasting Service (PBS) network. Their catalog is available FREE upon request.

5. WOMEN MAKE MOVIES FILM AND VIDEO CATALOG (Women Make Movies, Inc., 462 Broadway, Suite 500, New York, NY 10013): An invaluable source of gender-related and women's studies audio-visual material from which we drew heavily in this manual. All of the audio-visual materials in this catalog were made by women.

6. DIRECTORY OF WOMEN'S MEDIA (National Council for Research on Women, 47-49 East 65th St., New York, NY 10021): This guide includes brief descriptions not only of electronic media, but also of publishers, bookstores, libraries, archives, distribu-

tors, and mother media sources--all by, for and/or about women. It also contains an index of contact people for media resources and organizations.

In addition to these six comprehensive guides, instructors may also wish to consult university film center catalogs. University film centers listed in R. R. Bowker's EDUCATIONAL FILMS AND VIDEO LOCATOR publish annual catalogs that are usually available on request. Some centers also publish specialized media guides of their holdings (e.g., in sociology, in women's studies). An advantage of the university catalogs and guides over the Bowker guide is that they list current rental prices and policies.

Often instructors see a program on television that they would like to share with their classes. In such cases, the following information may be useful:

1. PBS PROGRAMMING: If you are interested in a program that has aired on PBS, keep in mind that PBS may or may not have distribution rights for it. To get specific rental or distribution information about a program aired by PBS, contact (in the order given) PBA Video Marketing at 800-424-7963 or PBS Programming at 703-739-5276. PBS also publishes a catalog of videos it has available for rent or purchase. To obtain a copy of the catalog, write to PBS, 1320 Braddock Place, Alexandria, VA 22314.

2. OTHER TELEVISED PROGRAMS: To find out where to rent or buy programs you have seen on TV or to pay for a license to use legally your own off-air video cassette recording outside your home. contact the programming department of the station or cable channel that aired the program. When you call, give the date the program was aired and full title (including the series title, if appropriate). Ask who has the rights to the program, because you are interested in renting it/buying it/obtaining an "off-air license" to show your own copy. The station itself will rarely be able to provide you with a copy or the right to use your own copy outside your home, but it should be able to give you a phone number or an address to obtain such rights. Several phone calls may be needed to track down the source and occasionally-- especially when the programming is extremely current--no copies or rights may yet be available.

In addition to the resources we have provided here, the media director of your university or local library may be able to offer further information and suggestions.

CHAPTER ONE

Multiple Choice:

1. The difference between sex and gender is that:
    * a.   the former is biologically determined, whereas the latter is socially constructed.
      b.   the former refers to masculinity and femininity, whereas the latter refers to a set of genetically determined traits.
      c.   the former is socially constructed, whereas the latter is biologically created.
      d.   none of the above; there is no difference between sex and gender.

2. Which of the following is not a component of "sex/gender systems"?
      a.   a sexual division of labor
      b.   the social regulation of sexuality, including positively and negatively sanctioned behavior
      c.   the social construction of gender categories on the basis of sex
    * d.   historical and cross-cultural acceptance of gender expectations

3. A sex/gender system in which men dominate women and that which is masculine is more highly valued than that which is considered feminine is called a:
      a.   matriarchy
      b.   gynearchy
    * c.   patriarchy
      d.   feminocracy

4. A paradigm is:
      a.   the social construction of gender categories
    * b.   a school of thought that provides a framework for a scientist
      c.   objective standards used to judge scientific findings
      d.   a universal view of scientific phenomena

5. A structural functionalist maintains that:
      a.   rapid social change is desirable
      b.   work done in the home is valuable and important
    * c.   biological differences have led to differing gender roles
      d.   all of the above

6. The structural functionalist perspective is problematic be cause it neglects:
   a. the structural causes of gender inequality
   b. the importance of social learning in gender development
   c. the consequences of gender inequality in society
 * d. both a and c above

7. The differential valuing of one sex over the other constitutes:
   a. ethnocentrism
 * b. sexism
   c. heresy
   d. functionalism

8. The feminist perspective maintains that:
   a. the world exists as an orderly social system
 * b. gender is socially created
   c. socialization plays no role in gender acquisition
   d. nature is unimportant in the acquisition of gender

9. Feminist researchers:
   a. focus on the experiences of women to the exclusion of those of men
   b. often use research methods that allow subjects self-expression
   c. examine differences between the behavior of men and the behavior of women
 * d. both b and c above

10. Feminist researchers reject:
 * a. the notion of value-free science
   b. scientific standards in research
   c. the inclusion of value judgments in scientific research
   d. the role of subjectivity in empirical research

11. From the feminist perspective, the consequences of sexism:
    a. are identical for all groups of women and men
    b. impact only on women
 * c. are made worse by other forms of oppression, including racism and heterosexism
    d. are not as bad as they used to be, thanks to the efforts of the women's movement

12. The feminist perspective is sometimes criticized for:
    a. failing to be empathetic to research subjects
 * b. engaging in structural determinism
    c. ignoring the concept of "power" in the sexual division of labor
    d. not acknowledging the importance of nature in gender acquisition

13. In her review of sociological literature, Lyn Lofland found that:
    a. women have different goals and ambitions than men do
    b. men's speech patterns are accepted as normative while women's are viewed as deficient
    c. most sociological studies were conducted by men
    * d. urban sociologists focused on settings which were male dominated

True/False:

14. Women constitute more than one half of the world's working population, but receive only 10% of the world's income.
    * a. true
    b. false

15. The term "gender" is a biological term meaning either male or female.
    a. true
    * b. false

16. Patriarchy is not a universal system.
    * a. true
    b. false

17. The most powerful members of a society usually are those who control the largest share of societal resources and the means of physical force.
    * a. true
    b. false

18. Feminist research is generally accepted as unbiased and "value- free".
    a. true
    * b. false

19. Feminist sociologists focus exclusively on the problems of women in society.
    a. true
    * b. false

20. The authors of your book have adopted the functionalist perspective.
    a. true
    * b. false

Essays:

21. Define the term "patriarchy." What is its relationship to gender?

22. Why is the feminist paradigm important for an understanding of gender acquisition?

23. Feminist social scientists have been critical of traditional research on gender. Specifically what are their criticisms? Identify and explain each of them.

24. Compare and contrast the feminist and structural functionalist perspectives. Discuss their positions on the biological influences of gender.

25. A national health agency is planning a study of the relationship between psychological depression and alcohol consumption. Representatives from the agency will visit bars and taverns in various neighborhoods throughout the United States and ask people drinking there to complete a questionnaire on their emotional state and their drinking habits. Evaluate this study from a feminist perspective.

Classroom Activity/Take-Home Assignment:

In an effort to encourage your students to recognize the values inherent in their own perspectives, ask them to write or state their position briefly on a current social issue of particular relevance to them (e.g., abortion, AIDS). Then ask them to explain and defend the position that is counter to their own. Finally, ask the students to specify the value biases that are inherent in each of the positions they have presented.

Film Suggestions:

1. Men and Women: After the Revolution -- interviews with twelve people from diverse backgrounds who discuss how changes brought about during the 1960s and 1970s affected their lives as women and men and their relationships. An excellent catalyst for classroom discussion. (58 minutes; available from: Fanlight Productions, 47 Halifax Street, Boston, MA 02130.

2. Gender: The Enduring Paradox -- explores the subject of gender in U.S. society by focusing on the formation of gender identity in childhood as well as socially-constructed notions of masculinity and femininity. (60 minutes; available from: PBS Video, 1320 Braddock Place, Alexandria, VA 22314

3. Rate It X -- looks at sexism in the United States as it's manifested in various areas (advertising, porn shops). Focuses on gender stereotyping and how specific gender stereotypes reinforce negative conceptions of women and sexuality. The filmmakers argue that sexism becomes rationalized through commerce, religion, and social values. This film is certain to generate classroom discussion and debate, but instructors should view it first before showing it in class, since some may find it offensive. (53 minutes; available from: Women Make Movies, 462 Broadway, Suite 500, New York, NY 10013).

4.   Pink Triangles -- explores the problems of prejudice, discrimination, and oppression primarily by focusing on hetero-sexism and homophobia, but also considers the historical and contemporary persecution of various racial, religious, and polit-ical groups. The film shows how members of minority groups are singled out as "different," "abnormal," or "inferior" and become the victims of a scapegoat mentality. (35 minutes; available from: Cambridge Documentary Films, P.O. Box 385, Cambridge, MA 02139.

Two films that are useful for illustrating the intersection of sexism, racism, and social class inequality are:

5.   Latina Women -- compares the lives of Latinas living in the United States with those living elsewhere in North America and in Latin America. The film considers the myths and mystique of machismo among Latinos today who, like others, increasingly are in two-income families and need shared child-rearing responsibil-ities. The film also profiles as Latina feminist activist. (26 minutes; available from: Films for the Humanities and Sciences, P.O. Box 2053, Princeton, NJ 08543).

6.   Japanese-American Women: A Sense of Place -- shows some of the conflicts experienced by Japanese-American women as they confront sexist as well as racist stereotypes. The film consid-ers, through the words of Japanese-American women, the sexist stereotypes of Asian women as exotic, docile, and polite. At the same time, the film considers the racist stereotype of Japanese-Americans as "model minorities." An underlying theme in the film is the problem of being "different" in the sense that these women often feel that they fit into neither Japanese nor American culture. (28 minutes; available from: Women Make Movies, 426 Broadway, Suite 500, New York, NY 10013).

Resources:

1.   The Center for Research on Women at Memphis State University is an excellent source of teaching and research materials on gender and, in particular, the intersection of gender, race, and social class. The center publishes a quarterly newsletter and has bibliographies, research papers, and curriculum materials for sale. For further information, contact: Center for Research on Women, Clement Hall, Memphis State University, Memphis, TN 38152.

2.   "An Inclusive Curriculum: Race, Class, and Gender in Socio-logical Instruction," edited by Patricia Hill Collins and Marga-ret L. Andersen, is a good source for syllabi and other teaching materials. It is available from: The American Sociological Association Teaching Resource Center, 1722 N Street N.W., Washington, D.C. 20036. ASA also has a sex and gender division, which, among many other activities, publishes a newsletter.

3.. The National Council for Research on Women (Sara Delano Roosevelt Memorial House, 47-49 E. 65th Street, New York, NY

10021) "is a coalition of seventy-five centers and organizations that support and conduct feminist research, policy analysis, and educational programs." The Council publishes several useful directories: "A Directory of National Women's Organizations," "A Directory of Work-in-Progress and Recently Published Resources," A Directory of Women's Media" (see the note about using films and videos at the beginning of this manual), and "The NCRW Directory Series," which includes a women's mailing list directory, a directory of international research centers, and a directory of opportunities for research and study.

4.   The Sociologists' Lesbian and Gay Caucus (SLGC) has five major objectives: to encourage unprejudiced sociological research on lesbians and gay men and their social institutions; to provide a forum for current research, teaching methods and materials, and professional issues relevant to homosexuality; to monitor anti-gay ideologies in the distribution of sociological knowledge and to investigate practices oppressive to lesbian and gay men; to oppose discrimination against gay and lesbian sociologists in employment, promotion, tenure, and research situations; and to maintain a social support network among its members. SLGC publishes a very informative newsletter. For information, write to the SLGC at P.O. Box 8425, Ann Arbor, MI 48107-8425.

Two other organizations to contact:

5.   The National Women's Studies Association, University of Maryland, College Park, MD 20742; and

6.   Sociologists for Women in Society, c/o Dr. Catherine Berheide, Department of Sociology, Skidmore College, Saratoga Springs, NY 12866.

There are numerous electronic forums to tap into for information on a wide range of gender-related topics. One of the best ways to get started in identifying those that are most useful to you is to peruse the women's studies electronic archives, which is available on the University of Maryland gopher. Anyone on gopher can gain access to the archives:

    After logging in, at the % prompt type: telnet gopher

    At the next prompt, type: gopher

    To access the archives, you must move through a series of menus. When the first menu appears, move the cursor to #11 (Other) and enter. Another menu will appear; move the cursor to #6 (University of Maryland) and enter. On the third menu, enter #4 (Educational Resources). On the fourth menu, enter #3 (Academic Resources/Topics). Finally, on the fifth menu, enter #9 (women's Studies Resources).

The electronic archives contain various files. You can mail any file back to yourself electronically by simply typing m. A box will then appear into which you will need to type your email

address. The file will then appear with the rest of your regular
email.

Joan Korenman's compilation (see the introduction to this manual)
notes that USENET is also a good source of electronic forums,
containing hundreds of news groups, including soc.feminism,
soc.women, and soc.men. All the news groups are public and open
to both women and men; all focus on discussions of gender relations and gender-related topics. Korenman suggests that since
there are different ways of accessing USENET, depending on the
system one is using, individuals wishing to gain access should
seek the advice of the computer support personnel at their institutions.

To obtain a compilation of gay, lesbian, bisexual, and transsexu-
al email lists, Korenman also recommends the following:

    Send the message: GET LESBIGAY LISTS WMST-L

    to: LISTSERV@UMDD

    or to: LISTSERV@UMDD.UMD.EDU

CHAPTER TWO

Multiple Choice:

1. Which of the following statements is NOT correct?
    a.   typically a person is born with 46 chromosomes
    b.   one set of chromosomes is referred to as the sex
         chromosomes because it plays a primary role in
         determining the sex of the fetus.
    c.   genetically normal females have two X chromosomes
 * d.   the mother's genetic contribution determines the sex of
         a child

2. All embryos are sexually bipotential (anatomically
    identical) until:
    a.   the third month of development
 * b.   the sixth week of development
    c.   the 28th week of development
    d.   none of the above; embryos are never sexually
         bipotential

3. The hormone testosterone is important in the development of
    the male fetus because it:
    a.   causes the degeneration of the female duct system
    b.   promotes the formation of the external genitals
    c.   promotes the transformation of indifferent gonads into
         fetal testes
 * d.   promotes the further growth of the male (wolffian) duct
         system

4. Which of the following suffer from adrenogenital syndrome
    (AGS)?
    a.   individuals who possess the sex chromosomes of normal
         males (XY) but are born with the external genitalia of
         females
    b.   individuals who have only one sex chromosome, an X
    c.   individuals in whom sexual differentiation is incomplete
 * d.   individuals who have the internal reproductive organs
         of females but whose external genitals are masculinized

5. Studies of AGS girls indicate that:
    a.   they are significantly more aggressive than non-AGS girls
 * b.   they appear to be more "tomboyish" than non-AGS girls
    c.   they show less interest in motherhood and marriage than
         non-AGS girls
    d.   they express a greater interest in dolls and dresses
         than non-AGS girls

6. Individuals who have the condition "androgen-insensitive syndrome" are:
    a. sometimes referred to as XY females
    b. are typically raised as females
    c. express a lesser interest in dolls, motherhood and dresses than genetically normal females
  * d. both a and b

7. Individuals with 5-alpha-reductase deficiency:
    a. typically are reared as boys, even though externally they appear to be girls
    b. have little difficulty changing their sex and gender identities at puberty when their external genitalia change
  * c. usually are recognized as "different" at birth and are socialized differently than "normal" boys
    d. behave masculinely throughout childhood because of exposure to prenatal testosterone

8. Turner's syndrome (XO) is caused by:
  * a. nondisjunction during the first meiotic division after fertilization
    b. over-exposure to prenatal testosterone
    c. under-exposure to prenatal testosterone
    d. none of the above

9. Individuals with Turner's syndrome:
    a. tend to be "tomboyish" girls
  * b. exhibit an exaggerated femininity in their behavior and personalities
    c. have a confused gender identity owing to the lack of a second chromosome
    d. tend to be overly aggressive

10. Men with Klinefelter's syndrome are at an increased risk of developing emotional and interpersonal problems most likely because:
    a. they do not secrete enough testosterone to adequately regulate their behavioral drives
    b. the possession of an extra sex chromosome directly produces abnormal behavior in males
  * c. of the difficulties involved in trying to cope with the physical abnormalities associated with this chromo-somal abnormality
    d. they do not produce sperm

11. XYY syndrome:
    a. has been shown to be directly related to violent be-havior
    b. is strongly associated with criminality
  * c. has been found disproportionately among institutional-ized males
    d. increases the likelihood of aggressive behavior

12. In the Money and Ehrhardt research on hermaphrodites, the most important variable for the development of gender identity was:
    * a.   the sex label given the individual by parents and family
      b.   the presence of testosterone in the blood stream
      c.   the chromosomal sex of the child
      d.   the individual's sexual anatomy as indicated by the genitals

13. Studies of prenatal mishaps:
      a.   are suspect because they must rely on data from very small, atypical samples
      b.   suggest that one's gender identity develops independently of one's chromosomal make-up
      c.   are subject to observer biases
    * d.   all of the above

14. Oversimplified summary descriptions of masculine men and feminine women:
      a.   are called sex roles
    * b.   are called gender stereotypes
      c.   usually have positive consequences for both sexes
      d.   rarely carry connotations of normality vs. abnormality

15. Scientists frequently measure dependency in terms of:
    * a.   separation anxiety
      b.   verbal ability
      c.   infant's activity
      d.   aggression

16. In their review of dependency research, Maccoby and Jacklin concluded that:
      a.   11 month old females were more dependent on their mothers than were 11 month old males.
      b.   females were generally more independent than males as children
    * c.   there is insufficient evidence to support the theory that girl infants are more dependent than boy infants
      d.   none of the above

17. Which of the following statements are true with regard to studies of aggression?
      a.   Most researchers use an objective measure of aggression, and thus do not rely merely on their perceptions
    * b.   there are no sex differences in aggression among infants, as measured by activity level
      c.   sex differences in aggression among adults are undisputed
      d.   the most popular argument for sex differences in aggression is based on progesterone levels

18. Kemper's research indicates that:
    a. there is a causal relationship between elevated testosterone and aggressive behavior
    b. illustrates how biology may be affected by social factors
    c. testosterone levels vary as a result of changes in an individual's social dominance or status
    d. all of the above
  * e. only b and c above

19. Hormone research on sub-primate mammals reveals that:
  * a. abnormally high levels of a variety of sex hormones may increase aggressive behavior.
    b. manipulation of hormones in early development has no effect on adult aggressive behavior.
    c. only females are affected by variations in hormone levels, not males
    d. all of the above

20. With regard to sex differences in visual abilities, which of the following statements is FALSE?
    a. infants' eye movements and length of time infants look at a visual stimulus are indicators of ability
    b. Maccoby and Jacklin found no differences for newborns
  * c. no significant differences are found until people reach their mid 20's
    d. no significant differences are found until adolescence

21. Research on infant sex differences in vocalization indicate that:
    a. boys are more vocal than girls
    b. females vocalize to inanimate objects, while males vocalize to human faces
    c. such differences can be found consistently across all societies
  * d. any observed differences may be due to mothers talking to their infant daughters more than infant sons

22. Research on infant sex differences tends to suffer from all of the following weaknesses EXCEPT:
    a. the confounding factors of the infant's physical and emotional states
    b. observers tend to know the sex of the child they are watching
    c. invalid measures of the traits or behaviors in question
  * d. none of the above, i.e., all of the above are weaknesses in this research

23. In tasks involving visual perception:
    a. males tend to be field dependent
  * b. females usually are field dependent
    c. it is better to be field independent because this approach to problem-solving is more complex
    d. all of the above

11

24. Research on men's and women's brains indicates that:
    a. males are right-brain dominant; males are left-brain dominant
    b. males are left-brain dominant; females are right-brain dominant
    c. men's and women's brains are identical
  * d. males' and females' brains may develop or be structured differently

25. Research on the biological bases of sexual orientation:
  * a. suffers from serious methodological weaknesses that calls its findings into question
    b. provides strong evidence that homosexuality is caused by structural differences in the brains of homosexuals
    c. are unilaterally denounced by gay men and lesbians
    d. has been given little attention by the media

26. All of the following are methodological weaknesses in the extant research on the "gay brain" EXCEPT:
    a. the use of brains from individuals who died from AIDS or who had a history of sexually transmitted diseases
  * b. the use of extremely large samples
    c. the exclusion of lesbians from the studies
    d. the failure to test the alternative hypothesis that particular forms of sexual behavior may change the structure and organization of the brain

27. Research on the social psychological causes of PMS indicates that:
  * a. negative expectations of and attitudes toward the experience of menstruation may precipitate a variety of physical and emotional symptoms
    b. negative mood changes do not appear to be related in any significant way to stressful external events
    c. debilitating symptoms associated with the menstrual cycle are psychosomatic
    d. cyclical mood swings are exclusively a female experience

28. Scientific studies of premenstrual syndrome (PMS):
    a. provide conclusive evidence that PMS is a gynecological disease
    b. demonstrate that the job troubles of a majority of women are due to menstrual changes
    c. indicate that PMS can be cured with regular injections of sex hormones
  * d. provide inconclusive evidence about the causes, consequences, and treatment of PMS

29. In her review of research conducted on the treatment of PMS, Dr. Judith Abplanalp found that a successful treatment of PMS was:
   * a.   placebos
     b.   vitamin B6
     c.   progesterone
     d.   testosterone

30. Research indicates that the incidence and severity of post-partum emotional disorders is directly related to:
     a.   a sharp drop in the secretion of the hormone progester-one following childbirth
     b.   the amount of social support available to new mothers
     c.   the amount and type of environmental stressors, such as housing and financial problems, to which new mothers are exposed
   * d.   all of the above

31. Biological reductionism is:
     a.   An environmental disease
     b.   the long term effects of progesterone on laboratory rats
   * c.   the tendency to reduce all sex differences to the level of biological imperatives
     d.   the direct relationship between hormones and sex differences

True/False:

32. Studies of prenatal mishaps indicate that the development of a masculine or feminine gender identity occurs independently of the presence of XX or XY chromosomes.
   * a.   true
     b.   false

33. According to Maccoby and Jacklin, female infants experience more separation anxiety than male infants.
     a.   true
   * b.   false

34. Scientists have proven that infants' activity level is a valid measure of aggression.
   * a.   true
     b.   false

35. Research indicates that children who are highly active as infants tend to display more aggressive behavior as young-sters or adults.
   * a.   true
     b.   false

36. Based on Maccoby and Jacklin's research, we know that one of the most consistent findings on infant sex differences is that males show greater interest in visual stimuli than females.
   a. true
   * b. false

37. Adult males perform better than females in solving visual-spatial problems.
   * a. true
   b. false

38. In regard to sound and vocalization, scientific research shows more similarity than difference between the sexes.
   * a. true
   b. false

39. Scientific research has proven that there is a direct relationship between brain lateralization and sex that predisposes males and females to behave differently.
   * a. true
   b. false

40. There is no empirical evidence that the brains of homosexuals may be structured differently than the brains of heterosexuals.
   a. true
   * b. false

41. Research indicates that the incidence of PMS varies cross-culturally.
   * a. true
   b. false

42. The greater the social isolation experienced by a new mother, the greater the likelihood that she will experience post-partum depression syndrome.
   * a. true
   b. false

Essays:

43. Discuss AGS, Turner's syndrome, and androgen-insensitive syndrome and what they teach us about gender?

44. Summarize this chapter's findings on sex differences in infants with regard to dependence; aggression; and visual and verbal abilities.

45. What is brain lateralization (or hemispheric asymmetry) and what does it have to do with gender?

46. Discuss the debate within the homosexual community regarding research on the biological bases of sexual orientation.

47. Explain the term premenstrual syndrome (PMS) and discuss how popular acceptance of this syndrome could both help and hinder the status of women?

48. Using your knowledge of sexual differentiation during fetal development, prenatal mishaps and brain lateralization, argue for or against this statement: Biological factors, not cultural ones, are responsible for specific gendered behaviors and sex differences.

49. What is meant by a "transformative account of gender development"? What is the potential for such a perspective to improve our understanding of the interaction of biology and and culture in the formation of gender?

Classrooms Activity/Take-home Assignment:

Before assigning Chapter 2 to your students, ask them to explore their own beliefs about sex differences and differences in sexual orientation by answering true or false to each of the following statements:

1. Toddler girls are more dependent on their mothers than toddler boys are.
2. Girls are naturally more talkative than boys are.
3. Boy babies are more aggressive than girl babies.
4. The differential organization of men's and women's brains causes them to behave differently from one another.
5. The differential structure of the brains of homosexuals and heterosexuals causes them to behave differently from one another, including but not limited to their sexual behavior.
6. The work performance of females is negatively affected by their menstrual cycles.

For each statement, ask the students to explain or provide the rationale for their answers. Students may then check their answers and examine their assumptions about gender differences and differences in sexual orientation as they read the chapter.

Film Suggestions:

1. Woman and Man -- a segment from "The Human Animal" series, examines the myth and reality of differences between women and men. (52 minutes; available from: Films for the Humanities and Sciences, P.O. Box 2053, Princeton, NJ 08543).

Also available from Films for the Humanities and Sciences:

2. The Sexual Brain -- examines sex differences in brain structure and functioning (28 minutes);

3.   Sex Hormones and Sexual Destiny -- explores not only the
controversy of sex differences in human brains, but also the
ways in which sex hormones may affect our behavior (26 minutes).

Also of interest are:

4.   Science and Gender with Evelyn Fox Keller -- a segment from
the "World of Ideas" series, this program looks at the life,
work, and views of Evelyn Fox Keller. Keller discusses discrimination against women scientists as well as how gender plays a
significant role in the language scientists use to describe their
work. (30 minutes; available from: PDS Video, 1320 Braddock
Place, Alexandria, VA 22314).

5.   Growing Up and Liking It -- an award-winning video that
explores with humor as well as a critical eye first menses and
the menstrual cycle. Through interviews with women of various
ages and cultural backgrounds, the film considers how this normal
biological functioning of a woman's body came to be enshrouded in
taboo and superstition. Women themselves recount the impact that
various experiences associated with menstruation had on their
everyday lives as well as their images of themselves and women
generally. (28 minutes; available from: Filmakers Library, 124
East 40th St., New York, NY 10016).

Resources:

1.   National Organization of Gay and Lesbian Scientists and
Professionals: For information, write to P.O. Box 91803, Pasade-
na, CA 91109.

2.   Association for Women in Science: For information, contact
the Association at 1522 K Street, NW, Washington, DC 20005.

3.   bionet.women-in-bio is a USENET news group for women in
biology. To subscribe, one must access USENET (see Resources,
Chapter 1).

CHAPTER THREE

Multiple Choice:

1. With regard to the archaeological record, which of the
   following is NOT true about the problems that archaeologists
   confront in reconstructing history?
   a.   for some periods, a fossil gap exists
   b.   archaeological finds are relatively sparse and fragmentary
   * c.   bone and stone eventually decay
   d.   the fossil record available does not provide an adequate
        picture of populations that once inhabited the earth

2. According to the traditional reconstruction of prehistory, which
   of the following was a result of bipedalism?
   a.   men hunted buffalo
   b.   our ape ancestors were able to spend much time in trees
   c.   men walked on four feet
   * d.   anatomical changes occurred including the narrowing of the
        pelvis

3. According to the feminist reconstruction of prehistory, the most
   significant social bond among our early human ancestors was that
   of:
   * a.   mother-offspring
   b.   father-offspring
   c.   husband-wife
   d.   mother-daughter

4. Man the Hunter theory is criticized for its:
   a.   biological reductionism
   * b.   ethnocentrism
   c.   simplification
   d.   indoctrinism

5. The authors of your textbook criticize traditional "Man the
   Hunter" theory for being androcentric. By this they mean that
   it:
   a.   judges other cultures by Western standards
   * b.   overlooks female contributions to evolutionary history
   c.   places too much emphasis on the role of bipedalism in human
        evolution
   d.   relies solely on the fossil record for evidence of how
        humans have evolved

6. The traditional reconstruction of prehistory maintains that the division of labor by sex developed as a result of:
 * a.   women's unique capacity to bear children
    b.   men's and women's erotic attraction to one another
    c.   men's unique capacity to hunt animals
    d.   all of the above

7. According to the feminist reconstruction of prehistory, the first human technology was probably:
 * a.   slings for carrying dependent offspring
    b.   tools for improving communication
    c.   weapons for warfare
    d.   weapons for slaying animals

8. The difficulty in linking archeological data with a specific sex is that gender attribution:
    a.   emphasizes household production to the neglect of public activities
    b.   overemphasizes the question of whether a sexual division of labor has always existed
    c.   deemphasizes public economic activities while focusing primarily on household activities
 * d.   is based on culture- and time-bound assumptions about what males and females do

9. Both the traditional (Man the Hunter) theory and the feminist theory of prehistory agree that:
 * a.   bipedalism led to significant changes in the relationship of an early mother to her offspring
    b.   meat comprised a significant portion of the early human diet
    c.   humans descended from the "killer apes" who moved into savanna regions as tropical rain forests receded
    d.   the sexual division of labor was adaptive

10. Regarding sociological research on chimpanzees, which of the following is FALSE?
    a.   females often initiate sexual activity and may choose one or more mates
 * b.   the largest male is usually dominant and has advantages over others
    c.   chimpanzees live in flexibly organized communities
    d.   a rigid hierarchical structure does not exist within the group

11. Studies of chimpanzees show that:
    a.   chimpanzees are pure vegetarians
    b.   chimpanzees do not share their food
 * c.   females usually share exclusively with their offspring
    d.   only males participate in food acquisition and preparation

12. With regard to the sexual division of labor, it appears that:
    a.   the work women do is devalued in nearly every known society
  * b.   there are almost no tasks universally assigned to men or women exclusively
    c.   there is rarely overlap in the activities performed by males and females
    d.   both a and b above

13. Anthropologist, Margaret Mead researched societies in New Guinea and found:
    a.   support for "Man the Hunter" theory of prehistory
    b.   that the role of women in prehistory has been traditionally ignored
    c.   that women have never participated in hunting and fishing
  * d.   that some cultures exist that contradict the Western construction of gender

14. Which of the following is a task from which women are universally excluded?
  * a.   metalworking
    b.   fishing
    c.   house building
    d.   boat building

15. Among foraging societies, which type is the least egalitarian?
    a.   Men hunt, women gather
    b.   Men and women communally hunt and gather
    c.   Men and women independently hunt, fish and gather
  * d.   Men hunt, women process the catch

16. Research on !Kung bush-living people indicates that:
    a.   men spend most of their time in the bush
    b.   men only are respected for their knowledge of the bush
  * c.   women and men share responsibility for raising children
    d.   there is no division of labor by sex

17. Cross-cultural research on foraging societies indicates that:
    a.   contemporary Western constructions of gender are not universal
    b.   the Man the Hunter theory is a valid explanation of gender evolution
    c.   a gendered division of labor does not always produce gender inequality
  * d.   both a and c.

18. Cross-cultural research on multiple genders:
    a. demonstrates the dichotomous nature of gender in all societies
  * b. illustrates how gender is a social creation
    c. shows that while cross-gendered behavior is tolerated in some societies, it is never regarded positively
    d. proves that cross-dressing among males is universally regarded as deviant

19. With regard to research on Navajo society, which of the following is NOT true about nadle?
    a. nadle had the social and legal status of women
  * b. the nadle status was only acceptable if applied at birth
    c. nadle had extensive sexual freedom
    d. nadle had the option of marrying someone of either sex

20. Studies of the Hua of Papua New Guinea show that:
    a. gender is dichotomous and permanent
    b. women are seen as socially acceptable only after giving birth to five children
  * c. gender can be fluid and changing rather than stable
    d. masculine people are regarded as invulnerable, but polluted

21. In developing their perspective of the evolution of gender, feminists have examined:
    a. primatology
    b. the archaeological record
    c. studies of contemporary foraging societies
  * d. all of the above

True/False:

22. Man the Hunter theory maintains that bipedalism led to the role of women as breadwinners.
    a. true
  * b. false

23. Feminist anthropologists do not regard bipedalism as an important historical adaptation.
    a. true
  * b. false

24. It is a fact that the genes of humans and orangutans are almost identical.
    a. true
  * b. false

25. Feminist anthropologists maintain that meat made up a relatively large portion of the early human diet.
    a. true
  * b. false

26. Sociologists have found that not every society has a division of labor by sex.
    a. true
  * b. false

27. Egalitarian gender relations are found today only in hunting and gathering societies.
    a. true
  * b. false

28. The authors of your text support Sigmund Freud's assertion that "anatomy is destiny."
    a. true
  * b. false

29. Gailey's research shows that among the Hua of Papua, New Guinea, men gradually lose their masculinity by passing it on to young boys during growth rituals.
  * a. true
    b. false

30. Research shows that among traditional Plains Indian groups, cross-dressed males were highly respected as the spiritual guardians of their societies.
  * a. true
    b. false

Essays:

31. Discuss the Man the Hunter theory of gender evolution and criticisms of the theory.

32. Compare and contrast Man the Hunter theory with the feminist reconstruction of prehistory. Which do you think is more credible? Why?

33. Explain why gynecentrism is as problematic as androcentrism in developing an understanding of the evolutionary development of contemporary gender relations? What kinds of questions will best add to our attempts to engender the past?

34. What do cross-cultural studies of foraging societies tell us about the gendered division of labor and stereotypical work roles of men and women?

35. Discuss multiple gendered societies and what they tell us about gender as dichotomous social categories.

36. Using your knowledge of foraging societies, multiple gendered societies and chimpanzee studies, explain why "anatomy is not destiny."

Classroom Activity/Take-home Assignment:

In this chapter we discuss evolutionary theories of gender. Much of the evidence we examine is archeological. To help students get a better understanding of the difficulties archaeologists confront, ask them to assume the role of "archeologist."

Their task is to reconstruct the early years of their childhood. Without the help of friends or family members, they must do this by searching for artifacts -- toys, photographs, and other keepsakes -- that may provide clues about the first few years of their lives. Then, using the gathered artifacts, students should write a brief reconstruction or description of what a typical day during these early years was like for them. Students should discuss how accurate they think their reconstructions are. They should also discuss the likely sources of inaccuracy in their reconstructions.

Film Suggestions:

1.   Margaret Mead -- a segment of the "Extraordinary Women" series from Films for the Humanities and Sciences, this brief video examines not only Mead's contributions to the field of anthropology, but also her defiance of the conventional gender expectations of her day. (12 minutes; available from Films for the Humanities and Sciences, P.O. Box 2053, Princeton, NJ 08543)

2.   Kypseli: Women and Men Apart, A Divided Reality -- a film based on an ethnographic study of gender relations in a small Greek village; "shows how the separation of the sexes and the principle of male dominance have become part of the village's most basic social structure, affecting the daily activities and thoughts of everyone there." (40 minutes; available from the University of California, Extension Media Center, 2176 Shattuck Avenue, Berkeley, CA 94704)

3.   Summer of the Loucheux -- examines the life of a young Native American woman and shows her in a variety of activities, including working beside her father and listening to the stories of her 93 year old grandmother; instructive not only for its examination of gender but also generational issues. (27 minutes; available from New Day Films, 853 Broadway, Suite 1210, New York, NY 10003)

Also available from New Day Films:

4.   Small Happiness -- an excellent documentary that examines the lives of women in a Chinese village. (58 minutes)

Resources:

1.   The Society of Lesbian and Gay Anthropologists (SOLGA): For information, contact Arnold Pilling, Department of Anthropology, Wayne State University, Detroit, MI 48202.

CHAPTER FOUR

Multiple Choice:

1. Gendercide:
    a. is the practice of deliberately killing females simply because of their sex
    b. appears to be increasing in some parts of the world, such as China and India
    c. is increasing due to the growing availability of technology, such as CVS
    * d. all of the above

2. Which of the following is NOT true about the process of socialization?
    * a. socialization occurs only during early childhood
    b. socialization is a way of transmitting society's norms
    c. socialization is a way of teaching society's values
    d. gender socialization is often a conscious effort

3. Research indicates that children are aware of their gender and adhere to gender stereotypes by the age of:
    a. four months
    * b. one year
    c. two years
    d. five years

4. Identification theory originated with the work of:
    a. Jean Piaget
    * b. Sigmund Freud
    c. Erik Erikson
    d. Nancy Chodorow

5. According to Freud's identification theory, children begin to model their same-sex parent during which stage of development?
    a. oral
    * b. phallic
    c. anal
    d. oedipal

6. According to Freud, which of the following is a consequence of "penis envy"?
    a. girls shift their love from their fathers to their mothers because they sympathize with others who have also been "castrated"
    b. girls identify with their fathers who possess the coveted penis
    * c. women never fully mature because they cannot overcome their feelings of sexual inferiority
    d. women learn to be good wives and mothers

7.   Which of the following is NOT a criticism of the identification theory?
     a.   it contains a definite antifemale bias
     b.   we have no way to objectively verify the process of identification
     c.   it implies that gendered behavior acquired early remains fixed over time
   * d.   none of the above; all are criticisms

8.   In Chodorow's revision of identification theory, it is hypothesized that gender identification is more difficult for boys because:
     a.   they must model their behavior after a parent of the opposite sex
   * b.   they must psychologically separate from their primary caretaker and model themselves after a parent who is usually absent from their homes
     c.   they suffer from womb envy
     d.   their relationships with their mother lead them to put others' needs before their own

9.   According to social learning theory, reinforcement leads to gender acquisition because:
   * a.   children are rewarded for gender-appropriate behavior and punished for gender-inappropriate behavior
     b.   it extinguishes children's Oedipal complexes
     c.   it helps them organize the world around them
     d.   none of the above

10. The theory that children acquire gender through the process of reinforcement and by modeling their same-sex parent is referred to as:
   * a.   social learning theory
     b.   identification theory
     c.   gender schema theory
     d.   cognitive development theory

11. Which of the following is a criticism of the social learning theory?
   * a.   children have some knowledge of gender apart from what they learn from modeling
     b.   the notion of "reinforcement" is not scientifically valid because it cannot be observed
     c.   it is a fact that children do not create schema or mental categories
     d.   the theory depicts children as active creators of socialization messages

12. The basic principle of cognitive developmental theory is:
    a.   children acquire gender through modeling
    b.   children acquire gender during psychosexual stages of
         development
    c.   children passively acquire gender through reinforcement
  * d.   children acquire gender through their mental efforts to
         organize their social world.

13. Cognitive-developmental theory helps to explain children's
    a.   preferences for same-sex friends
    b.   preferences for sex-typed toys
    c.   expression of stereotyped ideas about gender
  * d.   all of the above

14. Creation of gender schema is an important element of which
    theory?
    a.   social learning theory
  * b.   cognitive-developmental theory
    c.   identification theory
    d.   gender schema theory

15. Sex is a useful schema for young children because
    a.   it is abstract
    b.   it does not depend on reinforcement to be learned
  * c.   it is concrete and obvious, thus appropriate to young
         children's level of mental maturity
    d.   both a and b above
    e.   none of the above

16. According to psychologist Sandra Bem, children use sex as a
    fundamental organizing category because
    a.   it is simple and obvious
    b.   models of both sexes are readily available
  * c.   sexual distinctions are emphasized in our society's culture
    d.   none of the above; Bem does not agree that children use sex
         as an organizing category

17. The belief that males and females are not only fundamentally
    different, but also that sex is a central organizing prin-
    ciple for the social life of a society is called:
    a.   gender acquisition
  * b.   gender polarization
    c.   gender identification
    d.   gender reinforcement

18. Metamessages:
  * a.   lessons implicit in a society's culture about what is
         important, what is valued, and what differences are
         significant in that society
    b.   are the results of, not contributors to, gender social-
         ization
    c.   derive from the work of Sigmund Freud
    d.   develop in adulthood, once individuals have acquired
         their sex and gender identities

25

19. Studies of parents' reactions to the sex of their newborn children indicate that:
    a. gender socialization begins immediately after birth
    b. children in American society are born into a culture that shows some preference for males
    c. parents of girls are likely to handle their babies more than parents of boys
    d. all of the above
  * e. only a and b above

20. Studies of parental treatment of infants show that:
    a. parents engage in the same forms of physical contact with both their sons and daughters
    b. parents respond in the same way to boy and girl babies' cries for attention
  * c. parents elicit more motor activity from their sons
    d. none of the above

21. Research indicates that sex differences in young children's communication styles are likely due to:
  * a. differences in adult's responses to boys' and girls' communication attempts
    b. differences in the children's race and social class
    c. innate biological differences between boys and girls
    d. none of the above; there are no sex differences in children's communication styles

22. In examining the contents of children's rooms, sociologists have found that:
  * a. boys have more vehicular toys than girls
    b. girls have more books and musical instruments than boys
    c. neither a nor b above
    d. both a and b above

23. Most children's toys on the market today:
    a. are gender neutral
    b. easily cross gender lines
  * c. foster different traits and abilities in boys and girls
    d. encourage boys to be creative and girls to be competitive

24. Recent content analyses reveal that books for preschoolers:
  * a. contain roughly equal numbers of male and female characters
    b. depict both male and female characters as active and independent
    c. can no longer be considered sexist due to the efforts of publishers who have issued guidelines to help authors avoid sexism
    d. now have a female as a central character roughly 50% of the time

25. Comparisons of children's books written and illustrated by
    African Americans and white Americans reveal:
    a.   books written and illustrated by white Americans give
         female characters the greatest visibility
    b.   books written and illustrated by white Americans de-
         pict female characters as competitive and persistent
    c.   books written and illustrated by African Americans
         give female characters the greatest visibility
    d.   books written and illustrated by African Americans
         depict female characters as competitive, persistent,
         emotional, active, nurturant, and aggressive
  * e.   both c and d above

26. The success of publishers' efforts to produce nonsexist
    children's books may be limited because:
    a.   authors have refused to comply with publishers' guidelines
    b.   children naturally develop gender stereotypes regardless of
         what they see in their books
  * c.   adults who read the books to the children assign gender
         labels to gender-neutral characters
    d.   all of the above

27. Research on early peer group socialization indicates that:
    a.   young children have difficulty working cooperatively
         in sex-integrated groups
  * b.   children's same-sex peers are powerful socializers
    c.   young boys tend to interact in smaller peer groups
         than young girls do
    d.   girls receive greater criticism from their peers for
         gender inappropriate behavior than boys do

28. Hale-Benson's research on gender socialization in black
    families indicates that:
  * a.   black children of both sexes learn to be more independent
         and self-reliant than their white peers
    b.   black males are taught to accept matriarchal values
    c.   black females learn to reject motherhood in favor of work
         outside the home
    d.   there are no differences in gender socialization by race

29. Your authors emphasize that with regard to gender socializa-
    tion, race/ethnicity is an important variable because:
  * a.   the identity development of racial/ethnic minorities
         reflects the particular features of their own culture
    b.   the self-concepts of racial/ethnic minorities are not
         influenced or affected by their devaluation by the dominant
         white culture
    c.   racial/ethnic socialization consistently parallels that of
         the dominant culture in terms of gender stereotypes
    d.   both a and b above
    e.   both a and c above

30. Research on the relationship between social class and gender
     socialization:
     a.   has demonstrated conclusively that gender stereotyping
          decreases as social class increases
     b.   proves that gender stereotyping increases as one moves up
          the social class hierarchy
     c.   shows that there is no relationship between social class and
          gender stereotyping
  * d.   indicates that while social class appears to influence child
          rearing practices, race/ethnicity has a stronger effect

True/False:

31. Studies show that while most Americans prefer sons as first-
     borns, they prefer daughters to outnumber sons.
     a.   true
  * b.   false

32. According to Freud, "womb envy" is the underlying reason for
     men's need to dominate women.
     a.   true
  * b.   false

33. Research indicates that boys receive harsher penalties for
     cross-gendered behavior than do girls.
  * a.   true
     b.   false

34. A criticism of cognitive-developmental theory is that the
     theory does not put enough emphasis on the role of culture
     in gender socialization.
  * a.   true
     b.   false

35. As children get older and their cognitive systems mature,
     they also grow more inflexible about gender-specific activi-
     ties.
     a.   true
  * b.   false

36. According to Bem, the lens of gender polarization is incor-
     porated into the socialization process from birth:
  * a.   true
     b.   false

37. Mothers provide more stereotyped descriptions of their new
     borns than fathers do.
     a.   true
  * b.   false

38. According to the authors of your text clothing does not play
     a significant role in gender socialization.
     a.   true
  * b.   false

39. There has been no improvement in the number of female
    characters in preschoolers' books since 1972, when Lenore
    Weitzman did her research on this topic.
    a.   true
    * b.   false

40. Gender neutral books have solved the problem of sexism in
    literature by allowing individual readers to label the
    characters as they choose.
    a.   true
    * b.   false

41. Black children, in general, appear to be less independent
    and self-reliant than their white peers.
    a.   true
    * b.   false

42. The Hale-Benson study indicates that the black church is
    vital in socialization.
    * a.   true
    b.   false

Essays:

43. Explain identification theory and how it could be construed
    as "sexist."

44. Social learning theory involves both imitation and rein-
    forcement. Explain these two principles. What are the
    strengths and weaknesses of social learning theory as an
    explanation for gender acquisition?

45. What is cognitive-developmental theory? Discuss its
    strengths and weaknesses as a theory of gender acquisition.

46. Bem argues that gender acquisition involves the encultura-
    tion of three specific lenses. What are these lenses?
    Specifically, how do they each contribute to gender acqui-
    sition? What role do metamessages play in this process?

47. Discuss how children's environments play a role in gender
    socialization.

48. Explain how gender socialization differs by race/ethnicity
    and social class.

49. Is nonsexist socialization possible? Why or why not?

Classroom Activity/Take-home Assignment:

Ask your students to pay a visit to a local department store. Ask them to walk through the infant and toddler departments and take careful note of the differences in clothing available for boys and girls. The most obvious dissimilarity is that girls wear skirts and dresses and boys don't. But what about contrasts in style, in color or prints, or even in the texture of the fabrics? Are there any differences in the way the clothes are decorated and accessorized? Do any major themes emerge in the comparisons of the clothing? For example, what sorts of messages about masculinity and femininity come across subtly (or not so subtly) through the clothing? How might wearing these clothes affect the ways little girls and boys behave or the kinds of activities they are likely to pursue? Have the students compare their findings with those of the research discussed in this chapter. (With only slight revision, this assignment can also be done in toy stores with students comparing toys and toy packaging.)

Film Suggestions:

Three films which examine relations between parents and their children, especially fathers and their children are:

1.   Heroes and Strangers -- (29 minutes; available from New Day Films, 853 Broadway, Suite 1210, New York, NY 10003);

2.   New Relations -- (34 minutes; available from Fanlight Productions, 47 Halifax Street, Boston, MA 02130); and

3.   Fathers -- (52 minutes; available from: Filmakers Library, 124 East 40th St., New York, NY 10016).

Also of interest are:

4.   Dear Lisa -- a wonderful, entertaining film exploring the socialization of women, using home movies and interviews with thirteen women and girls (45 minutes; available from New Day Films, 853 Broadway, Suite 1210, New York, NY 10003).

5.   Black Mother, Black Daughter -- a film that focuses on the black community in Nova Scotia, Canada, and documents the culture and traditions transmitted across generations, especially from mothers to daughters. This film depicts a nurturing, active community in which family, church and community are intertwined and depend and support one another. (29 minutes; available from: Indiana University Center for Media and Teaching Resources, Bloomington, IN 47405).

For a fascinating look at the role of toys and the toy industry in gender socialization, see:

6.   Toying With Their Future -- (30 minutes; available from the National Film Board of Canada, 1251 Avenue of the Americans, 16th Floor, New York, NY 10020- 1173).

Resources

In addition to the resources presented in the text, instructors and students may also wish to contact: The Public Action Coalition on Toys, 38 West 9th Street, New York, NY 10011.

CHAPTER FIVE

Multiple Choice:

1.   With regard to the education of women, which of the follow-
     ing is FALSE?
     a.   women had access to formal education only after 1786
     b.   early education for women centered on women's domestic roles
     c.   in the nineteenth century, only upper-class women received
          formal educations
   * d.   the Young Ladies Academy of Philadelphia was the first
          institution that prepared women to assume public leadership
          positions

2.   Which of the following was NOT a consequence of the estab-
     lishment of free public schools in the 19th century?
     a.   the white female literacy rate rose in the northeastern part
          of the country
   * b.   females quickly moved into teaching positions in elementary
          schools where they received salaries comparable to their
          male counterparts
     c.   black literacy rates showed no substantial change in the
          early 1800's
     d.   female teachers outnumbered male teachers by 1860

3.   Which of the following is FALSE with regard to the early
     collegiate education of women?
     a.   It was argued that higher education was unhealthy for women,
          thus they were denied admission to many prestigious
          institutions
     b.   women were viewed as naturally less intelligent than men
          resulting in frequent denials for admission
     c.   in liberal institutions women were frequently treated
          differently than men and channeled into different areas of
          study
   * d.   only at elite universities such as Princeton and Harvard
          were women allowed to study business and law in the 19th
          century

4.   During the late 1940s and into the 1950s:
   * a.   the number of black women attending college increased
     b.   the number of black women attending college decreased
     c.   the number of white women attending college decreased
     d.   both a and c above
     e.   both b and c above

5.   Title IX of the Education Amendments Act of 1972:
     a.   was passed as a result of the efforts of the NAACP
     b.   prohibited racism in any federally funded educational
          institution
     c.   eliminated educational inequality on the basis of race
   * d.   prohibits sex discrimination in federally funded educational
          programs
     e.   applies only to athletic program in schools

6. Recent research in elementary school classrooms indicates that:
   * a. boys are given more help in finding and correcting errors than are girls
   b. boys and girls are equally praised for the intellectual quality of their work
   c. girls are given more detail for the completion of complex tasks because, in general, they require more guidance
   d. teachers provide challenges for girls more frequently than for boys because they are normally the better students

7. Students enrolled in special education programs:
   a. are fortunate in that the curricular offerings are rarely gender stereotyped
   b. tend to be boys because boys more often than girls have medically diagnosed learning disabilities
   * c. may have behavioral problems rather than learning problems
   d. all of the above

8. Research on teacher-student interaction shows that:
   a. black students, regardless of sex, receive more reinforcement for their academic achievements than white students do
   *b. black girls with high academic ability are often ignored by their teachers
   c. teachers, regardless of race, tend to reinforce girls, regardless of race, more than boys
   d. teachers reinforce children of their same race more than children of races different from themselves

9. Schools' formal curricula:
   * a. often provide sex-segregated vocational training programs
   b. have eliminated sex discriminatory programs because of the enactment of Title IX of the Education Amendments Act (1972)
   c. show little difficulty in integrating males into traditionally female classes
   d. reflect teachers' and parents' greater acceptance of allowing girls to be associated with masculine activities

10. Which of the following is NOT a consequence of sex separation in the classroom?
   a. working in same-sex groups becomes more comfortable than mixed-sex groups which can be problematic later in life for both men and women
   b. it prevents children from working cooperatively and denies them valuable opportunities to learn from the opposite sex
   * c. children of both sexes concentrate more fully on the tasks in front of them and less on things such as appearance or excellence in sports
   d. the reinforcement of gender stereotypes

11. Research on cooperative learning indicates that this approach:
    a. is highly successful in fostering positive relationships between girls and boys
    b. increases interracial friendships
    c. is especially helpful in mainstreaming students with disabilities
    d. all of the above
  * e. only b and c above

12. Traditionally, in children's textbooks:
    a. women and racial minorities are completely absent
    b. women are mentioned only in terms of traditional sex-typed roles
    c. children are taught that women and racial minorities have done little that is important
  * d. both b and c above

13. According to studies of boys and girls in secondary schools:
    a. girls on average score higher on their SATs
  * b. many girls expect a traditional future for themselves with regard to home and family
    c. high school sports are an important measure of popularity and prestige for both girls and boys
    d. girls' career aspirations seem to be directly related to academic achievement

14. A general rule of the status hierarchy of educators appears to be:
    a. "men teach, women manage or administrate"
  * b. "the higher up you go, the fewer women you'll find"
    c. "if you're female and you want to get ahead, choose education as a field"
    d. "women confront less discrimination the higher the level of education at which they teach"

15. Gay and lesbian high school students:
  * a. are at disproportionate risk of committing suicide
    b. show a disproportionately low rate of substance abuse
    c. receive extensive and visible support from school personnel
    d. tend to have more positive relationships with their parents than heterosexual teenagers do

16. Research reveals that boys do better in mathematics and science than girls do largely because:
    a. math and science are subjects that traditionally have been oriented toward males
    b. boys receive more encouragement from their parents in their study of mathematics and science
    c. boys receive more encouragement from teachers to pursue the study of mathematics and science
  * d. all of the above
    e. only a and b above

34

17. Horner's theory that women develop negative perceptions of themselves because they "fear success":
   a. has been widely accepted by both sociologists and psychologists
   b. has been replicated a number of times, and thus is a valid theory
   * c. has not been supported by consistent findings in replications of the original study
   d. should be disregarded because it has received no research support

18. In graduate education:
   a. women now outnumber men in traditionally masculine fields
   * b. men out number women in many fields that at the undergraduate level are female-dominated
   c. minority women outnumber white women in successfully completing degree programs
   d. minorities in general now outnumber whites in successfully completing degree programs

19. Sex segregation in particular fields of study appears to continue to persist because:
   a. most women "fear success" in these areas
   b. men are unwilling to enter female-dominated fields that typically carry low pay and low prestige
   c. women are discriminated against in male-dominated fields
   d. all of the above
   * e. only b and c above

20. Micro-inequities:
   a. are overt actions made frequently by male teachers
   * b. intensify in graduate school
   c. were first documented by Grove and Bell
   d. are directly prohibited by Title IX

21. Studies of full-time college and university faculty, show that:
   a. female university faculty members are paid the same salaries as males
   b. females are as likely to be tenured as males because of departmental quotas
   c. women are less likely to experience discrimination if they are black
   * d. none of the above

22. Research on differences in teaching styles and attitudes of female and male university and college faculty shows that:
    a. male faculty tend to focus on the student as the locus of learning
  * b. female faculty tend to use a more interactive style in the classroom
    c. male faculty tend to interact more with students outside the classroom setting
    d. female faculty discourage student participation in class

23. Female university faculty:
    a. are as likely to be tenured as men
  * b. are paid less than men, regardless of rank or tenure status
    c. are as likely as men to hold the rank of full professor
    d. are as likely as men to hold the rank of assistant professor or below

24. Female students:
    a. have greater opportunities to establish mentoring relationships than male students
    b. have greater opportunities to establish mentoring relationships than male students, only if they are also racial minorities
  * c. have fewer opportunities to establish mentoring relationships than male students
    d. have fewer opportunities to establish mentoring relationships than male students, only if they are also racial minorities

25. Which of the following statements about sexual harassment is FALSE?
    a. 2%-3% of female college students experience serious forms of sexual harassment
    b. most cases of sexual harassment go unreported
  * c. the most common types of sexual harassment involves students offering sex for grades
    d. sexual harassment of males by professors is relatively rare

26. An example of contrapower sexual harassment is when:
  * a. a male student propositions a female faculty member
    b. a female faculty member propositions a male student
    c. a male faculty member propositions a male student
    d. all of the above are examples of contrapower sexual harassment

27. A problem with "women-in" courses is that:
    a. the achievements of men are ignored
    b. the achievements of minorities are ignored
    c. there is no evidence that such courses have positive impacts on the students
  * d. they tend to view a few women as the exception to their kind and don't show women as central to social change

28. Curriculum revision projects designed to make the curriculum more multicultural and gender-inclusive:
    a. have received widespread support from most college and university faculty
    b. are protected by affirmative action laws from budget cut-backs and retrenchment
  * c. have positive impacts on students by diminishing stereotyped attitudes, increasing self-esteem, and broadening students' goals and understanding of their personal experiences
    d. have encountered little resistance from faculty because faculty typically welcome the opportunity to revise their course material

29. Gay and lesbian studies:
    a. developed in response to the failure of the traditional curriculum to examine the intersection of gender inequality and heterosexual privilege
    b. allows for a major shift in the intellectual life of gay and lesbian communities by promoting the entry of the university in those communities' cultural development
    c. challenges women's studies and feminist scholarship to promote greater ties with political and social movements
  * d. all of the above

True/False:

30. The hidden curriculum is as significant in conveying knowledge to students as the formal curriculum is.
  * a. true
    b. false

31. The primary reasoning behind the early education of women was to instruct them to be good teachers of civic virtue.
  * a. true
    b. false

32. By the year 1940, black men were receiving twice as many degrees from black colleges than were black women.
    a. true
  * b. false

33. Research shows that teachers typically interact differently with their male and female students.
  * a. true
    b. false

34. Boys outnumber girls in special education programs.
  * a. true
    b. false

35. According to a study of first graders, there is no measurable difference in children's gender-role perceptions between those who went to school with a male principal and those who went to school with a female principal.
   a.   true
 * b.   false

36. Curriculum materials and teachers frequently put a "ceiling" on girl's ambitions.
 * a.   true
   b.   false

37. The scarcity of males in traditionally female-dominated fields is mostly a result of discrimination.
   a.   true
 * b.   false

38. The gender gap in college and university faculty salaries has remained fairly stable during the last ten years.
 * a.   true
   b.   false

39. Between 1965 and 1990, the number of single-sex colleges increased substantially.
   a.   true
 * b.   false

40. Today there are signs that gender-inclusive curriculum revision programs will be instituted in most universities in the U.S.
   a.   true
 * b.   false

Essays:

41. What is a hidden curriculum and how does it differ from a formal curriculum?

42. How does primary and secondary education of children reinforce gender stereotyped behavior and expectations?

43. Discuss the importance of Title IX of the Education Amendments Act and problems that it did not address.

44. Discuss the pros and cons of gender separation in education.

45. To what extent are sex differences in math and science achievement attributable to innate differences between males and females and to what extent are they the product of environmental factors? How might the gender gap in math and science achievement be narrowed or closed?

46. Discuss the problems confronted by gay and lesbian youth in schools. Suggest ways that these problems might be effectively addressed.

47. With regard to gender and education, what are micro-inequities? Give two examples to illustrate.

48. Explain some of the problems associated with the higher education of men and women. Include in your discussion sexual harassment and women in graduate school as well as other related issues covered in this chapter.

Classroom Activity/Take-home Assignment:

This chapter makes the point that, although schools are officially charged with imparting certain knowledge and skills to the members of a society; knowledge and information NOT taught in school--ignored, in fact, in the formal curriculum--is significant too. The omission sends the implicit message that this material is unimportant. The information overlooked often concerns women and racial minority groups.

To illustrate this, give your students the following quiz:

1. When is George Washington's birthday?
2. When is Susan B. Anthony's birthday?
3. Who said, "Give me liberty or give me death"?
4. Who, when told that women are helpless weaklings, responded, "I have ploughed and planted and gathered into barns, and no man could herd me -- and ain't I a woman"?
5. What happened on December 7, 1941, "a day that will live in infamy"?
6. In what year did women win the right to vote?
7. Who was the first man to walk on the moon?
8. Who was the first American woman in space?
9. Who invented the light bulb?
10. Who invented the cotton gin?

The correct answers are: (1) February 22; (2) February 17; (3) Patrick Henry; (4) Sojourner Truth; (5) the day the Japanese bombed Pearl Harbor, which resulted in the United States entering World War II; (6) 1920; (7) Neil Armstrong; (8) Sally Ride; (9) Thomas Edison. Number 10 is a tough one. The answer is Eli Whitney and Catherine L. Greene. It appears that Greene hired Whitney as a tutor for her children, and together she and Whitney developed the cotton gin. In those days, though, the law prohibited women from owning property or controlling their earnings, so only Whitney could get a patent--and subsequently all the credit--for the invention.

In reviewing the correct answers with your students, emphasize that the important point to be made is not so much how many questions they answered correctly, but the content of the questions they answered correctly. Ask them to explain why they think they had difficulty with particular questions. (A good source of information for developing similar quizzes is THE BOOK OF WOMEN'S FIRSTS by P. J. Read and B. L. Witlieb (New York: Random House, 1992.

Film Suggestions:

The University of California, Extension Media Center (2176 Shattuck Avenue, Berkeley, CA 94704) offers three films in their "Sex Role Stereotyping in Schools" series:

1.   I is for Important -- examines stereotyping in social interactions and emotional expression (12 minutes);

2.   Hey! What About Us -- looks at physical activities in the classroom and on the playground (15 minutes); and

3.   Changing Images: Confronting Career Stereotypes -- presents a five-week project designed to change stereotyped career expectations of boys and girls (16 minutes).

PBS Video (1320 Braddock Place, Alexandria, VA 22314) offers two programs on "political correctness" on campus:

4.   Safe Speech, Free Speech and the University -- a panel discussion that examines is problem of "fighting words" on college campuses and controversial attempts to enforce "politically correct" speech through the enactment of speech codes (60 minutes); and

5.   Political Correctness/The Big Chill -- another discussion by "experts" of the dilemma of preserving First Amendment rights while also making campuses more multicultural (107 minutes).

Two videos that examine some of the problems of lesbian and gay youth are:

6.   First Dance -- the dramatization of a court case involving a Rhode Island gay teenager who was prohibited by his high school from attending the senior prom with his male date; especially useful as a catalyst for discussion of homophobia in schools, as well as how schools operate to enforce gender norms (19 minutes; available from: Fanlight Productions, 47 Halifax Street, Boston, MA 02130); and

7.   Gay Youth -- an award-winning documentary that explores the consequences of intense isolation experienced by many gay and lesbian teenagers. While this program discusses many of the negative effects of this isolation, including substance abuse, violence, and suicide, it also shows gay and lesbian youth with positive self-images who are actively combating homophobia.

Resources:

1.   One of the best sources of information on gender issues in education is the Project on the Status and Education of Women, 1818 R Street, NW, Washington, DC 20009. The project publishes a very useful newsletter, "On Campus With Women," as well as a number of research reports and other materials.

2.   The Women's Educational Act Publishing Center offers a wide variety of resources on most gender-related education issues. Contact: WEEA Publishing Center, Education Development Center, 55 Chapel Street, Suite 200, Newton, MA 02160.

3.   The American Sociological Association (1722 N Street, NW, Washington, DC 20036) also has a number of publications of interest available, including, "Equity Issues for Women Faculty in Sociology Departments."

4.   The American Association of University Women (1111 16th St., NW, Washington, DC 20036) conducts research on gender-related education issues and publishes valuable reports, including those referenced in Chapter 5 of the text.

5.   "Feminist Teacher" is a magazine devoted to disseminating information on alternative teaching tools and methods for covering such issues as sexism, racism, homophobia and other forms of oppression. It covers all grade levels--from preschool through graduate school--and a variety of disciplines. For information, write to: "Feminist Teacher," Wheaton college, Norton, MA 02766.

6.   From the American Council on Education (ACE) you can obtain a copy of the publication, "Sexual Harassment on Campus: A Policy and Program of Deterrence." This publication provides information on educating the campus community about sexual harassment and also offers guidelines for responding to sexual harassment complaints. Contact: the Publications Department, ACE, One Dupont Circle, Washington, DC 20036.

7.   Sociologists Against Sexual Harassment (SASH) has a moderated email forum to which one can subscribe. For more information, contact, Phoebe Stambaugh at Arizona State University: AZPXS@ASUACAD (bitnet) or AZPXS@ASUVM.INRE.ASU.EDU (internet).

See also the resources for Chapter 1.

CHAPTER SIX

Multiple Choice:

1. When a word that has a neutral connotation becomes debased over
    time or takes on a negative or derogatory connotation over time,
    the process known as _____ has occurred.
      a. symbolic annihilation
    * b. semantic derogation
      c. cultural lag
      d. linguistic substitution

2. "Linguistic sexism":
      a. refers to ways in which language devalues members of one sex
      b. involves ignoring women all together
      c. includes the smaller problem of semantic derogation
    * d. all of the above

3. Which is an example of linguistic sexism?
      a. "he/man" used specifically for males
      b. "Ms."
      c. "humanity"
    * d. "Mrs. John Smith"

4. Emphasis on the use of non-sexist language:
    * a. is necessary because language signifies and reinforces
          the status of individuals and groups within a particu-
          lar society
      b. downplays the more serious issues of the physical and
          economic oppression of women
      c. is trivial and misplaced
      d. both b and c above

5. Research on sex differences in communication styles indicates
    that:
      a. women interrupt others more than men do
      b. women talk more than men do
    * c. men are more successful in focusing conversations on topics
          they introduce
      d. men stand farther away from members of the opposite sex when
          speaking to them than women do

6. Men's nonverbal communication style is best characterized as:
      a. passive
      b. supportive
      c. empathic
    * d. dominant

7. Studies of same-sex conversations show that:
      a. men talk more than women
    * b. women's conversations may be described as cooperative
      c. women strive for conversational control
      d. men's conversations are friendlier than women's

8. According to the reflection hypothesis:
 * a. media content mirrors the behaviors, relationships, values, and norms most prevalent in a society
    b. the media actively shape and create culture
    c. the media are on the cutting edge of social change
    d. media content reflects the wishes of corporate sponsors who are rarely in tune with the views of the general public

9. The media practice of ignoring, trivializing, or condemning women is known as:
    a. semantic derogation
 * b. symbolic annihilation
    c. linguistic alienation
    d. blatant sexism

10. Research of daily newspapers indicates that:
 * a. women-centered events are usually reported as "soft" news
    b. symbolic annihilation is not a problem in the Washington Post and New York Times
    c. major newspapers are sensitive to the women's movement
    d. less personal information is given about women than men in news stories for reasons of protection

11. At major daily circulation newspapers:
    a. women remain underrepresented in the upper echelons of newspaper employment
    b. the number of women on newsroom staffs has increased significantly during the last two decades
    c. one of the most underrepresented groups on newsroom staffs in minority women
    d. all of the above

12. Research on popular women's magazines, shows that:
    a. many changes in the portrayal of women from 1949 to 1980
    b. having a happy family is not as important now as it was in 1950
    c. in the 1980s, the most popular theme was "getting and keeping a man"
 * d. femininity typically is defined by these magazines as a narcissistic absorption with oneself

13. Based on your authors' study of men's magazines, a general rule for the cult of masculinity appears to be:
    a. "real men are free and adventurous"
    b. "real men are self-consumed with their personal appearances"
    c. "real men are not concerned with getting and keeping a woman"
 * d. both a and c above

14. Television is an especially effective agent of socializa-
    tion because:
    a.   it is so widely available
    b.   no special skills are required to use it
    c.   all viewers, regardless of their personal or groups
         characteristics, are sent identical verbal and visual
         information
  * d.   all of the above

15. Research on prime-time television indicates that:
    a.   women are given more leeway in terms of their personal
         appearance than men are
  * b.   men are given more leeway in terms of their personal
         appearance than women are
    c.   women tend to be older and more mature than men
    d.   there has been a vast increase in the number of Hispanic
         women in central roles since 1970

16. On prime-time television:
    a.   women are typically depicted as problem-solvers
  * b.   female characters tend to be younger than male characters
    c.   minority males are cast in more favorable roles than
         minority females
    d.   female characters are more likely to hold the role of
         educated professional
    e.   the most favorable depictions are of old women

17. According to research by Press, television programs aired
    during the feminist period of TV programming:
    a.   depicted women as men's equals
    b.   depicted women as focused almost exclusively on their
         families
  * c.   increased the number of female characters who held
         positions in the male work world
    d.   increased the number of female characters on situation
         comedies to the detriment of female roles in action/
         adventure and dramatic prime-time series

18. Programming in the postfeminist period of television:
  * a.   portray strong or serious feminists negatively
    b.   typically show men performing household chores
    c.   frequently show women at work, on the job outside their
         homes
    d.   emphasize women's employment outside the home, but
         neglect their family problems
    e.   all of the above

19. When racial minorities appear on prime-time television:
    a.   it is typically in starring, rather than supporting
         roles
  * b.   they are typically cast in less prestigious occupations
         than white characters
    c.   they are more likely than whites to be cast as friends
         and neighbors
    d.   they are most likely to be cast as white-collar workers

20. With respect to television, homosexuals:
    a.   are rare on prime-time serials
    b.   typically are depicted as silly, vile, or victimized
    c.   have been portrayed more positively on public television than on commercial and cable television
  * d.   all of the above

21. Studies show that the greatest move toward equality of the sexes on television has taken place on:
  * a.   local news programs
    b.   network news programs
    c.   situation comedies
    d.   network mini-series

22. In television news programming:
    a.   women of color fare especially well in off-camera positions
    b.   female correspondents report equally as often as male correspondents
  * c.   the number of female correspondents among the top 50 increased between 1974 and 1992
    d.   minority female correspondents experienced a significant increase in their on-air reporting at the end of the 1980s.

23. With regard to music videos:
    a.   black men and women appear equally often in videos
  * b.   women are more often the aggressors than the victims of violence
    c.   white women are most frequently pictured dancing in the background
    d.   black women are frequently portrayed playing instruments

24. A general rule of music videos seems to be:
    a.   women and men are equally talented musicians and dancers
    b.   women are either sex objects or predators
    c.   men are aggressors or victims of aggression
  * d.   only b and c above
    e.   all of the above

25. The music videos of female artists today:
    a.   frequently appropriate for women the privileged experiences of men portrayed in most music videos
    b.   often depict a reversal of traditional gender roles
    c.   often represent a rejection of traditional gender stereotypes
    d.   increasingly address feminist issues, such as sexual harassment, women's control of their own sexuality, and reproductive freedom
  * e.   all of the above

26. The most common role for women depicted in advertisements
    is:
    a.   business woman
    b.   waitress
  * c.   housewife
    d.   teacher

27. With regard to voice-overs in advertisements:
    a.   90% of voice-overs are female
  * b.   studies show no differences in the persuasiveness of female
         and male voice-overs
    c.   studies show that male voices are more trusted by the public
         than female voices
    d.   as a result of reading sociological studies, more
         advertisers are using female voice-overs today

28. Research shows that advertisements that emphasize sex or
    that use women's sexuality to sell a product:
    a.   appeal to and are effective with men
    b.   are often appealing to teenagers of both sexes
    c.   are ineffective with a large segment of female con-
         sumers
  * d.   all of the above
    e.   only a and b above

29. Research on the impact of sexist media portrayals on peo-
    ple's actual behavior indicates that:
    a.   heavy television viewers tend to be more sexist than
         occasional viewers
    b.   heavy television viewers, particularly those who watch
         violent programs, tend to be less trusting and more
         alienated than occasional viewers
    c.   television advertising affects females' real-life
         aspirations
  * d.   all of the above

30. A study of television commercials by Geis and her colleagues
    indicates that:
    a.   television can have only detrimental effects on viewers
    b.   women's viewing of stereotyped commercials seemed to have
         little or no effect on their career aspirations
  * c.   nonstereotyped commercials can have a positive impact on
         women's aspirations
    d.   print media are more frequently detrimental to women's career
         aspirations than they are a positive influence

31. Current empirical evidence indicates that the relationship
    between viewing violent programs and engaging in actual vio-
    lent behavior is:
    a.   causal
  * b.   at least correlational
    c.   spurious
    d.   nonexistent (i.e., there is no relationship between
         these two variables)

32. It has been argued by some that watching violence reduces the likelihood that viewers will actually behave violently themselves, since the viewing allows them to release the tensions that may lead to real-life violence. This theory emphasizes the _____ effect of violent viewing.
   * a.   cathartic
     b.   catalytic
     c.   modeling
     d.   reinforcement

33. Researchers who emphasize the catalytic effect of viewing violence argue that:
     a.   violent viewing has the positive effect of inhibiting real-life violence
     b.   media violence teachers viewers to be violent through simple imitation
     c.   violent viewing rewards viewers for their own violent behavior
   * d.   viewing violent media depictions may prompt real-life violence, but it is not a sufficient cause in and of itself, since other variables intervene

True/False:

34. In a typical U.S. home, television viewing averages 35 hours a week.
   * a.   true
     b.   false

35. Research shows that efforts to alter practices of linguistic sexism in the media usually result in much confusion for the public.
     a.   true
   * b.   false

36. There is an increasing effort by major daily newspapers to recruit more gay men and lesbians to their newsroom staffs.
     a.   true
   * b.   false

37. Articles on occupational achievement are virtually identical in both women's and men's magazines.
     a.   true
   * b.   false

38. Racial minorities are more likely than whites to be cast as blue-collar workers and criminals on prime-time serials.
   * a.   true
     b.   false

39. Individuals with physical disabilities make up about 10% of prime-time television characters.
     a.   true
   * b.   false

40. Studies indicate that women of color are making even more progress than white women in local television news.
   a. true
 * b. false

41. Research indicates that the number of advertisements depicting men in decorative roles has doubled in recent years.
 * a. true
   b. false

42. The extent to which an individual viewer of violence is likely to imitate the violence that has been viewed is mediated by whether or not the violent model was rewarded for her or his violence.
 * a. true
   b. false

Essays:

43. What is linguistic sexism? Give two examples to illustrate.

44. What is symbolic annihilation and why is it a problem in the media? Using one type of media (newspapers, magazines, television, advertising), illustrate the problem of symbolic annihilation and speculate on its likely consequences.

45. Explain and critique the reflection hypothesis.

46. Compare and contrast the dominant themes in popular magazines for women and men.

47. Discuss television as a gender socializer. What are the images of men and women that are portrayed? Make sure to include information about music videos and news broadcasting.

48. How would you characterize the way that racial minorities, people with disabilities, and gay men and lesbians are typically portrayed on prime-time television? Discuss the likely impact of such portrayals on members of these groups.

49. Discuss gender messages in advertisements. Does sexism exist and if so, how can it be changed?

50. What are the three major theories of the relationship between the viewing of violence and real-life violent behavior? Provide an example to illustrate the central principles of each perspective.

Classroom Activity/Take-home Assignment

Invite your students to watch television for a couple of hours, but instead of looking at the programs, ask them to pay careful attention to the commercials. For each commercial they view, ask them to answer the following questions:

1. How many models are shown, and what is the sex and approximate age of each model?
2. How many models are members of racial minority groups? Which racial minorities are represented? How does their representation in the commercials compare with their representation in the general population?
3. What role (by sex, race, and age) does each model play (e.g., homemaker, physician)?
4. Are any of the models openly gay or lesbian and, if so, how are they portrayed?
5. Is there a background voice and, if so, is it a woman's voice or a man's voice?
6. Do the models have a real relationship to the product being advertised, or do they seem to be there purely as "decorations" -- that is, because they look good?
7. Are the role portrayals realistic? That is, would you expect people to behave this way in real life? Why or why not?
8. What promises about the product does the advertiser make? Put differently, does the advertiser try to sell you anything besides the product, such as a specific image? Do these images vary by sex, race, age, and sexual orientation?
9. Finally, try to imagine the female and male in the commercial reversed. Would the commercial make sense? Would the message be the same? Why or why not? What about young versus old models, or young women relative to older men and vice versa--would reversing these roles in a commercial allow the commercial to still make sense?

At the next class meeting ask your students to compare their results with those discussed in the chapter. (With a little modification, this exercise can also be done using magazine ads.)

Film Suggestions:

1. Sexism in Language -- looks at linguistic sexism by examin-ing specific examples of gender-biased language in song lyrics, everyday conversation, newspaper articles, etc; shows how gender-biased language, even when it is subtle, helps to shape the perceptions of both speakers and listeners (26 minutes; available from: Films for the Humanities and Sciences, P.O. Box 2053, Princeton, NJ 08543).

2. A Word in Edgewise -- also considers linguistic sexism, showing examples of bias and also ways to correct this problem

(26 minutes; available from Women Make Movies, 462 Broadway, Suite 500, New York, NY 10013).

3.   Newswomen -- Phil Donahue interviews several well-known female television news journalists, including Jane Pauley, Maria Shriver, Leslie Stahl, and Connie Chung, about how sexism and various gender-related issues impact on their careers and their personal lives.

Women Making Movies (462 Broadway, Suite 500, New York, NY 10013) also has available two excellent films on depictions of minority women in the media:

4.   Slaying the Dragon -- looks at media stereotypes of Asian and Asian American women (60 minutes); and

5.   And Still I Rise -- explores images of African American women in the media, focusing on myths of black women's sexuality (30 minutes).

Three programs on gender and advertising are:

6.   Model -- although now more than ten years old, this Frederick Wiseman documentary is still worth viewing for its inside look at the contrived world of advertising (129 minutes; available from Zipporah Films, 1 Richdale Avenue, Unit #4, Cambridge, MA   02140)

7.   Still Killing Us Softly -- a videotape of Jean Kilbourne's lecture on sexism in advertising, which is an up-date of her earlier production, Killing Us Softly (38 minutes; available from Cambridge Documentary Films, P.O. Box 385, Cambridge, MA   02139).

8.   Stale Roles and Tight Buns -- a good companion video to Still Killing Us Softly, this film examines images of men in advertising (29 minutes; available from OAIS, 15 Willoughby Street, Boston, MA 02135).

See also: Rate It X (Chapter 1)

Resources:

In addition to the Women's Institute for Freedom of the Press whose address is presented at the end of Chapter 6 in the text, there are other groups worth contacting for more information on gender and media. For example:

1.   Women on Words and Images, P.O. Box 2163, Princeton, NJ 08540.

2.   National Association of Hispanic Journalists, 1193 National Press Building, Washington, DC   20045.

3.   The Cultural Environment Movement (CEM) is a coalition of media, professional, labor, religious, environmental, health, women's and minority groups working for: a reversal of the concentration of control over media technologies; a halt to increasing media commercialization, conglomeratization, and globalization; an end to formula-driven homogenization of content; a more free, fair, and diverse cultural environment; and broad-based participation in cultural decisions that shape children's lives. Contact: George Gerbner, Chair, CEM, P.O. Box 31847, Philadelphia, PA 19104.

4.   "Challenging Media Images of Women" (P.O. Box 902, Framingham, MA 01701) is a feminist monitor of the media, including advertising.

5.   "The Women's Review of Books" is a publication of the Wellesley College Center for Research on Women, Wellesley, MA 02181. It is published monthly (except in August) and contains feminist reviews and review essays of books on a wide variety of topics, as well as interviews with authors and other types of articles. "The Women's Review of Books" makes for entertaining as well as informative reading.

6.   GENDER is a moderated email forum for the discussion of gender-related communications issues. To subscribe:

    Send the message: SUBSCRIBE GENDER <YOUR NAME> (your name should be your real name, not you email id)

    to: COMSERVE@RPITSVM (bitnet) or: COMSERVE@VM.ITS.RPI.EDU (internet); leave the subject line blank.

CHAPTER SEVEN

Multiple Choice:

1. According to Parsons, the role in which a family member is
    the economic provider and major decision maker is the:
       a.   expressive role
    * b.   instrumental role
       c.   nuclear role
       d.   status role

2. Which of the following is a problem of Parson's functional-
    ist perspective of the family?
       a.   his emphasis on the isolation of the nuclear family is
          unsubstantiated
       b.   men are portrayed negatively, as interested only in money
       c.   he legitimizes the fact that housework is unpaid labor
    * d.   both a and c above

3. Parson's description of the "isolated nuclear family"
    accounts for approximately ___% of U.S. households today.
       a.   80
       b.   50
       c.   30
    * d.   10

4. The idea that the work world is separate from the family is
    referred to as:
    * a.   the public/private split
       b.   the separation hypothesis
       c.   dualism theory
       d.   marginalization

5. Critics of the public/private split argue that:
       a.   the notion applies to full-time homemakers only
       b.   this dichotomy was accurate prior to 1900, but became
          increasingly erroneous
       c.   the idea pertains to men, but not women
    * d.   family members do not, in fact, experience these two spheres
          as separate

6. Stacey's research with working-class families revealed that
    these households often expand and contract in size as the
    needs of kin, including "ex-familia," change over time. She
    calls these households:
       a.   SNAFs
    * b.   accordion households
       c.   domestic partnerships
       d.   kinkeeping households

7. Research on the sexual activity of teenagers indicates that:
    a. by the age of 19, about 50% of males and females are
        still virgins
    b. a majority of teenagers say that premarital sex is
        "always wrong"
  * c. the gap between the sexual experience of young men and
        women has been closing during the last few decades
    d. the majority of young women report finding sexual in-
        tercourse pleasurable

8. The sexual double standard:
    a. is no longer common in U.S. society
    b. continues to be applied to males, but not to females
  * c. appears to be alive and well in U.S. society
    d. has disappeared as a result of the liberalization of
        attitudes toward premarital sex

9. Research on sexual orientation indicates that:
    a. sexual orientation is a dichotomous construct
    b. there is considerable consensus over the percen-
        tage of the U.S. population that is homosexual
  * c. sexuality is best characterized as fluid
    d. a much larger percentage of the population self-
        identifies as gay or lesbian than was originally
        estimated

10. The rate of teen pregnancy in the United States:
    a. is lower than in Europe
    b. is a reflection of the fact that U.S. teens are more
        sexually active than their European counterparts
  * c. is disproportionately high among racial minorities given
        their relative numbers in the population
    d. both b and c above

11. Research on teen mothers by Constance Williams shows that:
  * a. many young women become pregnant as a result of low
        self-esteem and the unavailability of alternative
        avenues for personal achievement
    b. the availability of welfare benefits is a major factor
        motivating young women to become pregnant
    c. most teen mothers can best be characterized a welfare
        dependent
    d. most teen mothers strongly wish to marry the fathers
        of their children, but the fathers strongly resist
        marriage

12. Contraceptives and abortion:
    a. are relatively recent inventions for the prevention and
        termination of pregnancy
    b. were illegal in the United States from the founding of the
        country until 1971
    c. are readily available to all women in the United States
        regardless of their socioeconomic position
    d. all of the above
  * e. none of the above

13. In Griswold v. Connecticut, the Supreme Court:
  * a.   ruled that the decision to bear a child is part of an
          individual's constitutionally protected right to privacy
     b.   extended the right to use contraceptives to unmarried persons
     c.   guaranteed women the right to an abortion during the first
          trimester of pregnancy
     d.   ruled that parents of minors must at least be informed of
          their child's intent to obtain an abortion

14. In Roe v. Wade, the Supreme Court ruled that:
     a.   women have an absolute right to terminate their pregnancies
          whenever they choose
     b.   the state may not interfere with a woman's right to obtain
          an abortion at any time during her pregnancy
  * c.   the state has no authority to prevent a woman from obtaining
          an abortion during the first trimester of her pregnancy
     d.   abortion is permissible only to safeguard a pregnant woman's
          health

15. With respect to new reproductive technologies:
     a.   the federal government has taken an active role in
          establishing strict regulations
  * b.   technological development has clearly outpaced the
          resolution of ethical dilemmas
     c.   research indicates that most procedures are safe and
          raise no public health concerns
     d.   both a and c above

16. Couples who are unable to conceive a child or to maintain a
     pregnancy also have difficulty utilizing other available
     options for obtaining a child because:
     a.   these options are often prohibitively expensive
     b.   religious, legal, or ethical problems prevent them from
          utilizing these options
     c.   most of these options carry serious health risks to both
          potential parents
     d.   all of the above
  * e.   only a and b above

17. In most states, the right to decide domicile legally belongs
     to:
     a.   a judge
     b.   the wife
  * c.   the husband
     d.   none of the above; most states no longer have domicile rights

18. The typical married woman today:
     a.   is a full-time housewife
  * b.   works outside the home
     c.   works outside the home only until her first child is born
     d.   none of the above

19. According to marital law, a husband's marital obligations are:
   * a.   the financial support of his wife
     b.   companionship services to his wife
     c.   contributing to the care of the household
     d.   agreeing to reside wherever his wife determines

20. Traditionally, sociologists have measured the distribution of power in families by examining:
   * a.   decision making by partners
     b.   the family's gross annual income
     c.   how much housework each partner performs
     d.   how many members of a household are employed outside the home

21. All of the following are criticisms of the use of decision making as a measure of marital power EXCEPT:
     a.   it treats all decisions as if they are of equal importance
   * b.   it overemphasizes the right to delegate responsibility for certain decisions to others
     c.   it does not take into account the division of household labor between marital partners
     d.   it overlooks the fact that one partner may act as the agent of the more powerful partner

22. Which of the following is a reason that housework commonly is not considered "real work"?
     a.   it is not paid work
     b.   it is produced for immediate consumption
     c.   it is privatized
   * d.   all of the above

23. Women who work outside the home:
     a.   have husbands who contribute significantly less time to household chores than the husbands of full-time homemakers
     b.   spend more time on housework than full-time homemakers
   * c.   continue to maintain primary responsibility for housework
     d.   have maids in the majority of cases

24. Which of the following is true with regard to the average husband's time spent on housework?
     a.   younger husbands tend to do more housework than older husbands
     b.   higher income husbands do less work than lower income husbands
     c.   the average husband spends 2 hours a week on housework
   * d.   husbands spend most of their housework time on non-daily, non-repetitive tasks

25. Research on househusbandry indicates that:
    a.   this lifestyle is growing in popularity
    b.   househusbands spend more time on housework than housewives
  * c.   most househusbands are either temporarily out of work or
         work out of their homes
    d.   this is the only effective means to equally divide household
         chores between spouses

26. All of the following have been offered by sociologists as
    reasons to explain why women continue to assume primary
    responsibility for the care of children EXCEPT:
    a.   women are naturally better suited to childcare than men
    b.   women are taught to mother from an early age whereas men are
         not
  * c.   men provide women with subliminal cues that cause them to
         engage in mothering behavior
    d.   the structure of work in our society leaves women and men
         with few other options

27. Recent research shows that women are _____percent of care-
    takers to elderly family members.
    a.   5
    b.   20
    c.   40
  * d.   75

28. With regard to marriage in the United States, which of the
    following is true?
    a.   one half will end within seven years
    b.   less than one half of marriages involve first time brides
    c.   the divorce rate is increasing
  * d.   both a and b above

29. In comparison with father-only households, female-headed
    households:
  * a.   are poorer
    b.   are fewer in number
    c.   enjoy fewer conflicts with job responsibilities
    d.   receive more help from relatives and neighbors
    e.   all of the above

30. In deciding custody, most courts today:
    a.   favor awarding sole custody to the mother
  * b.   favor joint custody arrangements
    c.   utilize the standard of maternal deference
    d.   have abandoned the best interests of the child stand-
         ard

31. The tender years presumption:
    a.   was adopted by the courts around the turn of the 20th
         century
    b.   holds that a young child needs to be with its mother
    c.   resulted in a dramatic shift in custody decisions
         against fathers and for mothers
  * d.   all of the above

32. Critics of the best interests of the child standard for awarding custody argue that:
   a. it unduly favors mothers regardless of how fit they are as parents
   b. it gives an unfair advantage to grandparents in hotly disputed custody cases
 * c. it is biased against women whose financial resources are not as great as those of their husbands
   d. it is biased against fathers who may have greater resources to promote and preserve the welfare of their children

34. No-fault divorce:
   a. requires that one partner sue the other for violation of the marriage contract
   b. has done little to alleviate the conflict and stress that characterizes most divorce cases
   c. is available only in a minority of states
 * d. has contributed substantially to increases in the number of female-headed households living in poverty
   e. all of the above

35. The poverty of many minority female-headed families is best characterized as:
   a. event driven poverty
   b. new poverty
 * c. reshuffled poverty
   d. subcultural poverty

36. Singlehood today is:
 * a. being prolonged largely in response to changes in the economy which have made it more difficult for young people to earn a wage adequate to establish an independent household
   b. increasingly becoming a permanent lifestyle for men, but not for women
   c. growing more popular because of the widespread image of the "swinging single"
   d. declining in popularity as evidenced by the steady drop in the median age of first marriage for both males and females

37. Those who have the greatest difficulty adjusting to divorce are:
   a. childless women
   b. women with grown children
 * c. women with children under six years old
   d. women with adolescent children

38. Studies of divorce indicate that one of the best predictors
    of the relative well-being of divorced women and men is:
    a.   their race/ethnicity
  * b.   the economic independence of the individual spouses
    c.   their educational backgrounds
    d.   none of the above

39. Analyses of gender differences in the divorce experience
    show that:
    a.   men in all socioeconomic groups are more likely than
         women to experience a drop in financial status follow-
         ing divorce
    b.   the most difficult period for men occurs prior to the
         couple's separation
    c.   women are quicker to remarry following divorce than men
         are
  * d.   following divorce, women adjust psychologically and
         emotionally better than men do

40. Research on widowhood indicates that:
    a.   being widowed impacts most negatively on women from
         low-income households
    b.   widowed men are more likely than widowed women to re-
         marry
    c.   widowed women adjust better to widowhood than widowed
         men
  * d.   all of the above

41. Widowhood:
  * a.   doubles the poverty rate of women
    b.   lowers the poverty rate of women in most socioeconomic
         groups
    c.   lowers the poverty rate of minority women only
    d.   has no impact on the poverty rate of women

42. Most heterosexual domestic partnerships in the United
    States:
    a.   are composed primarily of couples under 25 years old
    b.   last from 5 to 10 years duration
  * c.   end prior to the birth of children to the cohabiting
         partners
    d.   are composed of women and men who previously were
         married

43. Studies of homosexual relationships show that the majority of
    gay and lesbian couples:
    a.   are "out" about their sexual preferences
  * b.   enjoy especially high levels of dyadic attachment com-
         pared with the dyadic attachment of heterosexual cou-
         ples
    c.   engage in substantial role playing
    d.   model their relationships on those of heterosexual couples

44. In its Bowers v. Hardwick decision, the Supreme Court:
   a. outlawed discrimination against homosexuals
 * b. in effect gave its approval to discrimination against homosexuals
   c. extended the rights and obligations of the marriage contract to homosexual unions
   d. decriminalized specific sexual practices if engaged in by consenting adults.

45. Gay and lesbian domestic partners encounter the greatest acrimony and resistance to equal treatment in the area of:
   a. employment benefits
   b. health insurance coverage
 * c. parental rights
   d. privacy rights

46. Battery:
 * a. is the single major cause of injury to women in the United States
   b. occurs predominately among poor and working class couples
   c. is as likely to be perpetrated against husbands as it is against wives
   d. typically results in the arrest and conviction of the abusive spouse

47. Recent research indicates that those women who most quickly escape abusive marriages are:
   a. living near relatives who are willing and able to help them
   b. well educated
   c. employed outside the home or have high employment potential
   d. childless or have few children
 * e. all of the above

48. Research indicates that spouse abuse is most likely caused by:
   a. lack of education among abusers
   b. low income among abusers
   c. alcohol or drug abuse
   d. psychological maladjustment within abusers
 * e. none of the above

49. All of the following EXCEPT _____ are cultural factors that contribute to the high incidence of spouse abuse in the United States.
   a. a legal history that positively sanctioned wife beating
 * b. a high rate of mental illness among U.S. men
   c. commonly held attitudes of wife beating as acceptable behavior in marriage
   d. the notion of family privacy

50.	Research indicates that:
	a.	the relationship between alcohol abuse and domestic violence is causal
	* b.	excessive drinking is a contributing factor to domestic violence in that it serves to excuse or justify battering
	c.	the majority of batterers are alcoholics
	d.	there is no relationship between alcohol abuse and domestic violence

51.	Studies of mandatory or preferred arrest policies:
	* a.	indicate that arrest appears to be an effective deterrent only among batterers who have a high stake in conformity
	b.	show that such policies typically encourage women, especially minority women, to call the police when they are abused
	c.	show that such policies are most effective in protecting women who fight back against abusive partners
	d.	indicate that arrest is more effective than any other form of police intervention for deterring battering

52.	Gay men and lesbians who have been abused by their partners have difficulty leaving the abusive relationship because:
	a.	of the high level of dyadic attachment they have to their partners
	b.	they do not perceive the sources of help available to heterosexual battered women as being available to them
	c.	leaving an abusive partner would mean substantial financial loss which may or may not be recoverable through legal action due to institutionalized homophobia in the legal system
	* d.	all of the above

53.	Child abuse:
	a.	appears to be perpetrated by fathers more often than mothers
	* b.	occurs in a social context in which force is an apparent means to solve problems
	c.	tends to be overreported by neighbors who hear children crying
	d.	is a contemporary problem without historical antecedents

54.	National data show that about 19 percent of girls and 9 percent of boys in the United States are victims of sexual abuse by the time they turn 18; ____percent are abused by a relative.
	a.	less than 10
	b.	25
	* c.	40
	d.	63

60

55. Elder abuse:
    a.   has been more widely studied than either child abuse or spouse abuse
  * b.   appears to be most often perpetrated by an adult daughter or son who is caring for a parent
    c.   must be reported to the police in all 50 states
    d.   appears to be unrelated to other forms of domestic violence

56. Among the following, the group most likely to be at risk for elder abuse is:
    a.   men, aged 65 to 75
    b.   minority men
  * c.   women, aged 75 and older
    d.   minority women, aged 65 to 75

True/False:

57. Historically, a man's family was defined by law as his property just as his material possessions were.
  * a.   true
    b.   false

58. The majority of women with children under the age of 18 are full- time homemakers.
    a.   true
  * b.   false

59. The traditional nuclear family is the most common family form in the United States.
    a.   true
  * b.   false

60. Teens in the United States are more sexually active than their peers in Europe.
    a.   true
  * b.   false

61. The United States has the highest rate of teenage pregnancy of all Western industrialized nations.
  * a.   true
    b.   false

62. Women living in rural areas have more difficulty obtaining abortions than women in urban areas.
  * a.   true
    b.   false

63. It is now technologically possible for post-menopausal women to get pregnant and bear children.
  * a.   true
    b.   false

64. The majority of states in the U.S. now have laws that make surrogacy illegal.
    a.   true
  * b.   false

65. A homemaker today spends about as much time on household chores as a homemaker in the late 18th century.
  * a.   true
    b.   false

66. Although most two-earner couples say they support an equal division of housework, their practices do not reflect this belief.
  * a.   true
    b.   false

67. Race interacts with social class in affecting the amount of time husbands spend doing housework.
  * a.   true
    b.   false

68. A woman's power in the marital relationship increases with the birth of her first child.
    a.   true
  * b.   false

69. Egalitarian marriages tend to become more traditional in terms of the division of labor once children are born.
  * a.   true
    b.   false

70. Most fathers when given the opportunity prefer to take time off from work to be with their newborn infants.
    a.   true
  * b.   false

71. The percentage of children living with their fathers only has more than doubled since 1970.
  * a.   true
    b.   false

72. The median annual income of two-parent families is more than twice that of single-parent, female-headed households.
  * a.   true
    b.   false

73. Women are more likely than men to experience financial difficulties during widowhood.
  * a.   true
    b.   false

74. Most cohabiting couples decided to either break up or marry with in two years after they begin living together.
  * a.   true
    b.   false

75. Lesbian couples as a group appear to have more stable relationships than either heterosexual couples or gay male couples.
   * a.   true
     b.   false

76. Gay and lesbian couples may now legally marry in at least 5 states in the United States.
     a.   true
   * b.   false

77. A woman has a higher probability of being assaulted by her partner in their home than a police office has of being assaulted on the job.
   * a.   true
     b.   false

78. Many women who remain in abusive relationships for an extended period of time do not leave their batterers because they do not believe that they can adequately support themselves and their children.
   * a.   true
     b.   false

79. Research indicates that it is easier for lesbians and gay men to leave abusive relationships than it is for heterosexual women to leave such relationships.
     a.   true
   * b.   false

80. Unwanted or unplanned children are at especially high risk for abuse and neglect.
   * a.   true
     b.   false

Essays:

82. What is the public/private split? How accurately does it reflect family life in the United States? Provide specific examples to illustrate your argument.

83. Discuss the ethical problems raised by the new reproductive technologies. Suggest some ways in which these difficulties might be resolved. What are the implications of your suggested resolutions in terms of reproductive rights and freedom?

84. It has been argued that the decision to have a child is a public as well as a private one. Explain this statement by showing how various social, political, and economic factors impinge upon reproductive freedom in the United States.

85. Specifically how does the division of household labor affect the balance of power in a marital relationship?

86. What are the advantages and disadvantages for both women and men of the traditional gendered division of caregiving responsibilities in the home?

87. How do changes in marital status affect the respective economic statuses of women and men? How can we account for these gender differences?

88. Discuss the problem of institutionalized discrimination against homosexuals by examining specific examples of this problem. What effects does institutionalized discrimination have on lesbians and gay men?

89. What are the advantages and disadvantages for gay and lesbian couples of legal recognition through registration of gay and lesbian domestic partnerships?

90. "Might makes right" is a popular figure of speech in the United States. Show how it often applies in families by analyzing one of the forms of domestic violence discussed in your text.

Classroom Activities/Take-Home Assignments:

1.   Divide the class into pairs or small groups and ask each pair or group to write a marriage contract that covers all of what they believe to be significant issues in a marital relationship (e.g., the division of household labor, how money will be spent, family size, how children--if any--will be reared, etc.). Have the members of each pair or group discuss their contract with the rest of the class, indicating why they focused on the particular issues they did and some of the conflicts that arose, or that they think might arise, in negotiating these issues. Then ask them to compare their contracts with the marital laws in their state (or the state in which the college or university is located). Most students are quite surprised to learn that a contract such as the one they developed would not be upheld in court, and that they will have to live by the marital regulations of the state, regardless of whether or not these run counter to their personal wishes. (You will probably need to explain to the students the difference between a marital contract and a prenuptial agreement.)

2.   Ask your students to research their state's laws regarding the reporting and prosecution of child abuse and neglect, partner abuse, and elder abuse. Do the state (or local) laws covering domestic violence include protections for homosexual victims of partner abuse? Are these laws written in a gender-neutral manner? In some states, the laws are written explicitly to exclude

lesbian and gay victims from protection. Is this the case in their states? What resources are available specifically for lesbian and gay victims of domestic violence?

This project may be assigned as a library research project, but it is more effective if students are required to interview officials directly involved in dealing with these problems. The class may be divided into groups, one group assigned to interview police officers about how they respond to domestic violence calls and their typical methods of intervention, another group assigned to talk to social workers in the local office of family services about their intervention policies and the problems they face in monitoring domestic violence cases, a third group assigned to speak with the district attorneys and assistant D.A.s about how they prepare such cases for prosecution, a fourth group assigned to interview shelter staff, and so on. The field research approach to this project is especially useful in highlighting the homophobia gay and lesbian domestic violence victims face, as well as the myths about other forms of domestic violence that continue to impede all domestic violence victims in getting appropriate and effective help.

Film Suggestions:

Several films are available that examine intimate relationships, family structure, and caregiving:

1.   Love Stories (Part I: Women; Part II: Men) -- provides a fascinating contrast between women and men of various ages and backgrounds in how they perceive intimate relationships and the appropriate roles for women and men in those relationships. An excellent catalyst for classroom discussion (Part I is 40 minutes and Part II is 20 minutes; both available from: Cine Research Associates, 32 Fisher Avenue, Boston, MA 02120).

2.   Asian Heart -- a film about Asian "mail order" brides and the men who court them by mail and bring them to their own country (in this case, Denmark) because they believe these women will be more "old-fashioned" and accommodating than "liberated" Western women. Winner of the Margaret Mead Film Festival in 1987 (38 minutes; available from: Filmmakers Library, 124 East 40th Street, New York, NY 10016).

3.   Toward Intimacy -- through interviews with four women with disabilities, this film explores some of the problems these women have confronted in building fulfilling intimate relationships and in expressing themselves sexually; a moving and positive portrayal (60 minutes; Filmakers Library, 124 East 40th Street, New York, NY 10016).

4.   A Family to Me -- looks at four different types of families in order to dispel the myth that the only true family is the traditional nuclear family (28 minutes; New Day Films, 22-D Hollywood Ave., Hohokus, NJ 07423).

5   Things Your Mother Never Told You -- examines changes in women's lives as mothers during the last thirty years by exploring with forty women of various ages and backgrounds their perceptions about being a mother. Includes the stories of a physically challenged woman who raised a family despite her handicaps and a single woman who adopted a child (58 minutes; available from: Filmmakers Library, 124 East 40th Street, New York, NY 10016).

6.   Choosing Children -- also challenges stereotypes about what constitutes a family; this film examines the issues faced by women who become parents after coming out as lesbians (45 minutes; available from: Cambridge Documentary Films, P.O. Box 385, Cambridge, MA   02139).

Two other awarding-winning films on gay and lesbian families are:

7.   We Are Family -- (57 minutes; available from: Filmmakers Library, 124 East 40th Street, New York, NY 10016); and

8.   Not All Parents Are Straight -- (58 minutes; available from: The Cinema Guild, 1697 Broadway, New York, NY 10019).

Two additional films on caregiving are:

9.   When the Day Comes: Women as Caregivers -- for women discuss and demonstrate the stresses they confront in providing continuous care for an elderly loved one (28 minutes; available from: Filmakers Library, 124 East 40th St., New York, NY 10016); and

10.   Family Caregivers -- not only examines the difficulties involved in caring for ill and disabled loved ones, but also offers coping strategies (30 minutes; available from: Films for the Humanities and Sciences, P.O. Box 2053, Princeton, NJ 08543).

A number of excellent films are available on issues of reproductive freedom, especially abortion and new reproductive technologies. Among them:

11.   Abortion Clinic -- from the PBS series "Frontline," this video examines the decisions of four women, as well as the operation of a clinic where about 3,000 abortions are performed annually. Also included are the activities of anti-choice protesters. This is a valuable video in that it demonstrates nicely that actual abortion decisions are rarely, if ever, as clear-cut as both pro-choice and anti-choice advocates make them out to be. (52 minutes; available from: Fanlight Productions, 47 Halifax Street, Boston, MA   02130).

12.   Access Denied -- examines the curtailment of women's reproductive freedom within the context of anti-abortion demonstrations by Operation Rescue. The film focuses on growing community activism to reverse this curtailment as well as to mobilize

groups on the problems of racism and AIDS (28 minutes; available from: Women Make Movies, 462 Broadway, Suite 500, New York, NY 10013).

13. Back Alley Detroit -- an historical documentary that provides the post-Roe v. Wade generation with an education about what life was like for women with unwanted pregnancies before abortion was legalized. Rather than sensationalizing the subject, this film sensitively tells the stories of women from diverse backgrounds and circumstances who underwent illegal abortions. It also shows the efforts of many physicians, clergy, and health activists who sought to help these women and others like them (47 minutes; available from: Filmakers Library, 124 East 40th St., New York, NY 10016).

14. Motherless -- also recounts life in the pre-Roe v. Wade era but from a very different perspective: that of four children, now grown, whose mothers died from illegal abortions. This is a very powerful film; highly recommended (30 minutes; available from: Filmakers Library, 124 East 40th St., New York, NY 10016).

15. Mother's Day -- explores issues generated by technological advances that now allow postmenopausal women to bear children; includes many perspectives on a variety of questions, including whether this technology is beneficial to the offspring of these women as well as to society as a whole (52 minutes; available from: Filmakers Library, 124 East 40th St., New York, NY 10016).

16. On the Eighth Day -- is a two-part film that examines in-depth many of the social, economic, and ethical dilemmas posed by the new reproductive technologies (Part I, Making Babies, and Part II, Making Perfect Babies, each is 51 minutes; available from: Women Make Movies, 462 Broadway, Suite 500, New York, NY 10013).

17. Underexposed: The Temple of the Fetus -- combines drama and documentary to examine issues raised by the new reproductive technologies, but also traces the historical treatment of women's sexual and reproductive functions as "diseased" and in need of medical intervention. This film emphasized ways in which new reproductive technologies exploit women's bodies (72 minutes; available from: Women Make Movies, 462 Broadway, Suite 500, New York, NY 10013).

Women Make Movies (462 Broadway, Suite 500, New York, NY 10013) also has one of the best selections of films on lesbian relationships. Among them are:

18. Forbidden Love -- through interviews with ten lesbians, this films educates students about life for lesbians during the 1950s and 1960s (85 minutes);

19. Thank God I'm a Lesbian -- focuses on diversity within the lesbian community by exploring several lesbians' views on racism, bisexuality, sadomasochism, outing, and so on (55 minutes);

20. Women Like Us -- focuses on older lesbians (ranging in age from 50 to over 80); sixteen women tell their stories, including some of the difficulties they faced in coming out (49 minutes); a sequel, Women Like That, also is available and discusses with eight of these the ways that their lives have changed since Women Like Us was released in 1990.

21. Lifetime Commitment -- originally released in 1988 and updated in 1993, this film chronicles Karen Thompson's legal struggle to win the right to care for her partner, Sharon Kowalski (30 minutes).

Also on gay and lesbian relationships:

22. Silent Pioneers: Gay and Lesbian Elders -- an outstanding documentary that refutes not only many myths about aging, but also many myths about homosexuality, through interviews with eight gay and lesbian senior citizens. Also examines some of the special problems confronting elderly homosexuals. Winner of fifteen film awards in 1985 and 1986 (42 minutes; available from: Filmmakers Library, 124 East 40th Street, New York, NY 10016);

23. Out in Suburbia -- talks with eleven lesbians and in so doing dispels many myths about lesbians and the gay community; explores issues such as marriage, motherhood, and gender roles.

Finally, there are a number of excellent films and videotapes about domestic violence available, including:

24. Defending Our Lives -- the award-winning film that chronicles the terrifying circumstances that led each of four women to kill their abusive partners; documents the failure of the criminal justice system to protect these women from violence and their subsequent victimization by the system itself when they were imprisoned for defending their lives (40 minutes; available from: Cambridge Documentary Films, P.O. Box 385, Cambridge, MA 02139).

25. The Battered Woman -- interviews with seven battered wives and with expert panelists (e.g. a psychiatrist, a lawyer) explore the reasons for spouse abuse and solutions to the problem (60 minutes; available from: PBS Video Marketing, 1320 Braddock Place, Alexandria, VA 22314).

26. Generations of Violence -- examines the intergenerational hypothesis of family violence (that violence is learned in the family and passed on from one generation to the next). Includes interviews with abused children and abusive parents, as well as with professionals who work with victims and abusers (55 minutes; available from: Filmmakers Library, 124 East 40th Street, New York, NY 10016).

27. Sandra's Garden -- examines the problem of incest by chronicling the moving story of one woman who continue to heal and is helped in this process by her lesbian partner and other women in

her community (34 minutes; available from: Women Make Movies, 462 Broadway, Suite 500, New York, NY 10013).

28. Secret Sounds Screaming -- a sensitive examination of the sexual abuse of children and teenagers that focuses on the power dynamics of child sexual abuse by placing it in the context of race and social class (30 minutes; available from: Women Make Movies, 462 Broadway, Suite 500, New York, NY 10013).

See also: Black Mother, Black Daughter (Chapter 4); Fathers (chapter 4)

Resources:

1. For information on teen pregnancy, the problems of female-headed households, and young families, contact: the Children's Defense Fund, 122 C Street, NW, Washington, DC 20001. Also contact: the Child Welfare League of America, 440 First Street, NW, Suite 310, Washington, DC 20001.

2. For resources on reproductive freedom, contact: the National Abortion Rights Action League, 1101 14th Street, NW, 5th Floor, Washington, DC 20005; and the Center for Women Policy Studies, 2000 P St., NW, Suite 508, Washington, DC 20036. The latter organization also has publications available on new reproductive technologies.

3. There are several good resources for lesbian and gay domestic partnerships and parenting rights, including an email forum. To subscribe, send email to: domest-request@cs.cmu.edu

The National Center for Lesbian Rights (1663 Mission St., Suite 550, San Francisco, CA 94103) has published "Recognizing Lesbian and Gay Families: Strategies for Obtaining Domestic Partner Benefits." See also, "The Lesbian and Gay Parenting Handbook: Creating and Raising Our Families," written by April May and published by Harper Perennial; and "Partners: the Newsletter for Gay and Lesbian Couples," (P.O. Box 9685, Seattle, WA 98109).

The National Gay and Lesbian Task Force, 1517 U Street, NW, Washington, DC 20009, also has outstanding resources available on many aspects of gay and lesbian relationships.

4. Perhaps the best source of information on all aspects of domestic violence is the National Resource Center on Domestic Violence, 6400 Flank Drive, Suite 1300, Harrisburg, PA 17112-2778, (800-537-2238). The NRC provides comprehensive information and resources, policy development, and technical assistance. It is part of the Domestic Violence Resource Network. Also included in the resource network are:

a. The Battered Women's Justice Project (800-903-0111) which provides training, technical assistance and other types of resources through a partnership among three organizations: The Domestic Abuse Intervention Project of Duluth, MN (fax: 218-722-

1545) addresses the criminal justice system's response to domestic violence, including the development of programs for batterers; The National Clearinghouse for the Defense of Battered Women (fax: 215-351-0779) addresses battered women's self-defense issues and publishes a very informative newsletter, "Double-Time"; and the Pennsylvania Coalition Against Domestic Violence (fax: 610-373-6403) addresses civil court access and legal representation of battered women.

b.   The Resource Center on Child Protection and Custody (800-527-3223) which is housed in the National Council of Juvenile and Family Court Judges Family Violence Project (fax: 702-784-6628) and provides information, consultation, technical assistance and legal research related to child protection and custody issues within the context of domestic violence.

c.   The Health Resource Center on Domestic Violence (800-313-1310) which is housed in the Family Violence Prevention Fund (fax: 415-252-8991) and provides specialized information packets to improve the health care response to domestic violence. It also provides technical assistance and library services to support health care-based domestic violence training and program development.

Also a good source of information on all forms of domestic violence is the Family Violence and Sexual Assault Institute (1310 Clinic Drive, Tyler, TX 75701) which publishes the biannual newsletter, "Family Violence and Sexual Assault Bulletin." It is a good source for obtaining unpublished manuscripts on various aspects of domestic violence as well as sexual assault.

There are a number of groups that specifically address domestic violence in same-sex relationships. Contact, for instance, the Network for Battered Lesbians, Box 6011, Boston, MA 02114; and the New York City Gay and Lesbian Anti-Violence Project, 647 Hudson, New York NY 10014.

For information specifically on child abuse, contact: the National Committee for the Prevention of Child Abuse, 332 S. Michigan Ave., Suite 950, Chicago, IL 60604, which has chapters in many states.

There also is a family/intimate violence email forum. To subscribe:

    Send the message: SUBSCRIBE INTVIO-L <YOUR NAME> (remember that you should send your real name and not your email id)

    To: LISTSERV@URIACC (bitnet)   or: LISTSERV@URIACC.URI.EDU leave the subject line blank

CHAPTER EIGHT

Multiple Choice:

1. The Industrial Revolution was significant for women in the labor
    force because it resulted in:
    a.   bringing millions of women from "all walks of life" into the
         labor force
 * b.   bringing millions of women into the textile industry
    c.   bringing women the same jobs and pay as men
    d.   bringing wealthy women into the work force

2. Women's participation in the labor force rose most dramatically:
    a.   during the Depression
    b.   after World War II
    c.   after 1900
 * d.   during World War II

3. The increase of women's participation in the labor force
    after 1965 was a result of all of the following EXCEPT:
 * a.   government sponsoring of public day-care centers
    b.   the decreasing fertility rate
    c.   expansion of the service sector
    d.   new divorce laws

4. World War II was important for women's participation in the
    labor force for all of the following reasons EXCEPT:
    a.   it enabled women to hold jobs previously held only by men
    b.   minority women were given new job opportunities
 * c.   it changed forever the "normal" role of women as wives and
         mothers
    d.   women were paid wages that were equivalent to those of men

5. The degree to which men and women are concentrated in occupations
    in which workers of one sex predominate is known as:
    a.   dissimilarity index
    b.   collar segregation
 * c.   occupational sex segregation
    d.   human capital theory

6. The dissimilarity index:
    a.   compares the characteristics of women's and men's jobs
 * b.   is the proportion of workers of one sex that would have to
         change jobs in which members of their sex are under- repre-
         sented in order for the occupational distribution to be
         balanced
    c.   is the percentage of women who hold men's jobs
    d.   is higher in the United States than any other country in the
         world
    e.   both b and d above

7. With respect to occupational sex segregation:
    a. blue collar workers are less sex segregated than white collar workers
  * b. young workers are less sex segregated than older workers
    c. the higher the educational requirements for the job, the lower the sex segregation
    d. between 1960 and 1980, the majority of jobs in the U.S. became more sex-integrated

8. The labor market in the United States is best characterized as:
    a. equal relative to that of other industrialized countries
    b. professionally-oriented
    c. female dominated
  * d. a dual labor market

9. Which of the following is a consequence of workplace sex segregation?
    a. male-dominated occupations are usually more stressful than female-dominated occupations
    b. women are less susceptible to unemployment than men
    c. there is a decrease in productivity of industrial workers when men and women are kept separate
  * d. both men and women are likely to confront hostility in jobs that are non-traditional for their sex

10. In 1970, about 18 percent of communications operators were male, whereas in 1988, about 89 percent were male. This is an example of:
  * a. resegregation
    b. disaggregation
    c. tokenism
    d. establishment sex segregation

11. The majority of female physicians practice in just three medical specialities, whereas male physicians are concentrated in more lucrative specialities. This is an example of:
    a. resegregation
  * b. industry sex segregation
    c. establishment sex segregation
    d. all of the above

12. In highly segregated workplaces, the presence of a few "tokens" often prompts workers from the dominant group to exaggerate differences between themselves and the tokens. This is referred to as:
    a. resegregation
    b. appropriation
    c. mentoring
  * d. boundary heightening

13. In her study of men in female-dominated jobs, Christine Williams found that:
    a.   men experience greater negative treatment in these jobs than women do in male-dominated jobs
    b.   these men frequently encounter subtle pressure to not seek promotion or upward mobility in the profession
 * c.   these men receive preferential treatment in hiring and promotion
    d.   it is the numerical rarity rather than the social status of a token's group that determines a token's employment experiences

14. Which of the following is true of the sexual harassment that women experience in the workplace?
    a.   it rarely occurs
    b.   it has been eliminated by Equal Employment laws
 * c.   it is more pervasive in male-dominated jobs
    d.   it happens to one half of female employees in the U.S.

15. The male\female wage gap:
 * a. remained relatively stable between 1960 & 1990
    b. steadily narrowed between 1960 & 1990
    c. is expected to close completely by 2000
    d. exists for every job except female-dominated ones

16. Today, full-time, year-round female workers earn on average about _____ percent of what male workers do.
    a.   54
    b.   49
 * c.   76
    d.   87

17. Women and minority workers:
 * a.   are more likely than male and white workers to be hired as temporary workers
    b.   are less likely than male and white workers to be hired for part-time employment even though they wish to work full-time
    c.   tend to have as much likelihood of being hired for prestigious jobs as male and white workers do
    d.   tend to work year-round more often than male and white workers do

18. Our nations' welfare system:
    a.   encourages able-bodied men to remain unemployed
    b.   provides sufficient benefits to pull most recipients out of poverty
    c.   has steadily increased the benefits it provides
 * d.   is designed to enforce the norm of the traditional nuclear family, and women's place in it

19. The majority of the elderly poor are:
   a. women
   b. living alone
   c. members of racial minority groups
 * d. all of the above

20. The fastest growing segment of the homeless population is:
 * a. young families with dependent children
   b. young men, aged 18-24
   c. men, aged 65 and older
   d. women, aged 25-44

21. In her study of homeless women, Golden found that:
   a. experiences of domestic violence were relatively rare
      in the women's life histories
   b. few of the women exhibited symptoms of mental illness
   c. the primary reason for homelessness among the recent-
      ly homeless was loss of relationships
   d. homeless women have less difficulty than homeless men
      in obtaining paid employment

22. Which of the following is the best explanation for the
    gender gap in wages?
   a. women are more likely than men to work in jobs that require
      minimal levels of education
   b. women work fewer hours than men
   c. typically men are employed in full-time jobs and women are
      not
 * d. female-dominated occupations pay less than male-dominated
      occupations

23. The theory that women choose to invest less time than men in
     employment outside the home is known as:
   a. occupational segregation theory
   b. primary provider theory
 * c. human capital theory
   d. comparable worth theory

24. The more children a woman has the more likely she is to:
   a. choose not to work outside the home
 * b. work in a male-dominated occupation
   c. seek a job with rotating shifts
   d. feel welcome in a nontraditional job

25. Relative to other industrialized countries, the United
    States policy on child care:
   a. is more advanced
   b. is designed to provide fathers as well as mothers with
      parental leave time from their jobs
   c. benefits women, but not men
 * d. none of the above, i.e., the United States have no official
      child care policy

26. With respect to the relationship between education and wages, research shows that:
    a. a worker's years of schooling directly effects her or his wages, regardless of sex
  * b. sex differences in education are unrelated to the gender gap in wages
    c. educational attainment has a significant impact on raising women's wages, but the reverse is true for men
    d. educational attainment has a significant impact on the wages of minority men and women, but is unrelated to the wages of white men and women

27. Which is an example of "statistical discrimination"?
    a. hiring women to be construction workers
    b. hiring men to be nurses
    c. not hiring a "token" person
  * d. not hiring women in their child bearing years

28. All of the following are examples of the law's reinforcement of gender discrimination EXCEPT:
    a. Bradwell v Illinois
    b. Muller v Oregon
  * c. Executive Order 11246
    d. EEOC v Sears, Roebuck and Co.

29. Anti-discrimination laws have been largely unsuccessful in improving women's employment status because:
    a. the laws themselves contain inherent weaknesses
    b. the courts hold considerable discretionary power to interpret the laws in various (and often contradictory) ways
    c. the organization of work in our society is itself sexist
  * d. all of the above

30. Comparable worth refers to a policy in which:
    a. men and women are given equal pay for equal work
    b. men and women are hired for the same jobs
  * c. men and women are paid equally for jobs of similar value
    d. men and women are regarded as colleagues in different departments of their workplaces

31. Recent economic and political changes in the former Soviet Union and Eastern Europe:
    a. have resulted in improved job opportunities for women in those countries
    b. seem to have made blatant sexism permissible
    c. have eliminated many of the opportunities that women previously enjoyed under socialism
    d. all of the above
  * e. only b and c above

True/False:

32. Female-dominated occupations, regardless of educational requirements, pay substantially less than male-dominated occupations.
    * a.   true
      b.   false

33. Gay men who hold female-dominated jobs enjoy preferential treatment in hiring and promotion.
      a.   true
    * b.   false

34. Statistics indicate that men are more likely than women to hold jobs that pay the minimum wage.
      a.   true
    * b.   false

35. "Home-based child care," given in the home by an unlicensed provider, accounts for the majority of child care in the United States.
    * a.   true
      b.   false

36. The courts have ruled that sexual harassment is a form of employment discrimination under Title VII of the Civil Rights Act.
    * a.   true
      b.   false

37. The Equal Pay Act prohibits sex segregated employment and advocates the principle of "comparable pay for comparable work."
      a.   true
    * b.   false

38. Recent political and economic changes in the former Soviet Union has resulted in new legislation that outlaws all forms of sex-based discrimination.
      a.   true
    * b.   false

Essays:

39. Trace the history of women's labor force participation in the United States. What are some of the specific problems that have confronted women in the workplace?

40. Discuss and give examples of how minority women have been doubly disadvantaged in the workforce. Refer to wage gaps, occupational opportunities and anything else you find to be relevant.

41. Compare and contrast the effects of the glass ceiling with those of the glass escalator?

42. What are some of the myths about welfare recipients? Specifically, how does the welfare system reflect sexist stereotypes?

43. Explain why elderly women are more likely than elderly men to live in poverty.

44. How do men's and women's experiences of homelessness differ?

45. Your text discusses several remedies for lessening occupational sex segregation. Discuss these and indicate how they might be successful in addressing this problem.

46. Discuss the pros and cons of comparable worth as a solution to the gender gap in wages.

48. Discuss the strengths and weaknesses of legislation designed to prevent and remedy sex- and race-based discrimination in the workplace.

49. How have recent political and economic changes in the former Soviet Union affected the status of women in the new countries of the Commonwealth of Independent States?

Classroom Activities/Take-home Assignments

1. Often, college students cannot fully understand the constraints that are imposed by specific income levels because they are not responsible for the everyday expenses of running a household and providing for the needs of a family. This exercise is designed to foster that understanding.

Divide the class into several groups, each group representing a family with a particular income level (for example, a single-parent household headed by a thirty-five year old woman with two children, a girl aged six and a boy aged eighteen months, with a net income of $13,012 per year, compared with a two-parent family with two children with a net income of $42,514 per year. Median incomes for different types of families can be obtained by consulting the STATISTICAL ABSTRACT OF THE UNITED STATES which is fully referenced in the text). Each group should be given a copy of the "Family Budget Planner" included here. (This form was developed by the U.S. Department of Agriculture and Commerce to assist families in budgeting their incomes.) Have each group complete the budget for the family it has been assigned, planning either for a year or dividing the income and planning for one month. You will probably have to help with utility estimates and the like.

After the budget forms are complete, ask a spokesperson for each group to report to the class how it spent its money. Ask students to comment on specific problems they faced because of their available incomes.

2.   Students are often surprised when they learn about the salary differences between "men's jobs" and "women's jobs." To further illustrate the gender gap in wages and develop a discussion of the problem and its consequences, ask the class to look carefully at the list of occupations below and rank order them according to how much they think a worker who holds such a job should be paid (1 = lowest paid; 7 = highest paid). (The actual median earnings for each of the occupations can be found in the chapter.)

_____ airline pilot

_____ construction laborer

_____ teacher's aide

_____ bank teller

_____ truck driver

_____ police officer

_____ librarian

Ask the students what factors they took into consideration in developing their ranks--e.g., the level of skill required for each job, the degree of responsibility each job entails. To what extent did they consider the sex of workers who are most likely to hold such jobs? Although many students will argue that sex is irrelevant, they will learn in the chapter that the sex of the majority of workers holding a particular job is closely related to the level of compensation attached to that job. This exercise is useful for sparking discussions of the sexist assumptions underlying job evaluation systems.

3.   Many students are surprised to learn that men and women are charged different amounts of money for the same services or products. Several recent news programs have aired videotaped results of undercover investigations that have showed that men pay less to have their clothes dry-cleaned, get better deals when buying a car, and so on. Your students may want to do an undercover investigation of their own. One way of doing this is to ask for male and female volunteers to separately take an identical white shirt/blouse to a local dry-cleaner for laundering and subsequently compare the charges. In most locales, the male student's dry-cleaning bill typically will be 50 cents to $1.00 less than the female student's dry-cleaning bill, despite the fact that the garments cleaned were identical.

Film Suggestions:

New Day Films (853 Broadway, Suite 1210, New York, NY 10003) has several outstanding films available on gender-related work and economic issues:

1.   The Global Assembly Line -- examines the manufacture of many of the everyday items in our lives in "free trade zones" in developing countries where many of the employees are poorly-paid young women (58 minutes);

2.   With Babies and Banners -- tells the story of women's role in the Great General Motors Sit-down Strike of 1937 and how their activities were crucial in the successful drive for industrial unionism (45 minutes);

3.   Union Maids -- another historical documentary about women's union organizing activities during the 1930s (48 minutes); and

4.   The Double Burden: Three Generations of Working Women -- looks at the lives of three families, each with three generations of women who have always worked outside the home in addition to raising families; these families are of different races, social classes, and lifestyles (56 minutes).

Films for the Humanities and Sciences (P.O. Box 2053, Princeton, NJ 08543) also offers a number of films that focus on women and work:

5.   Problems of Working Women -- covers various difficulties women in the labor force who also have young children confront, especially child care (24 minutes);

6.   Sexual Harassment from 9 to 5 -- tells the stories of three women who experience sexual harassment on the job and how their lives were affected by these experiences (26 minutes);

7.   Women on Top -- examines the controversy over the effectiveness of feminine traits versus masculine traits in the business world and attempts to answer the question, Must a woman act like a man to be successful in the professional world? (20 minutes).

The Cinema Guild (1697 Broadway, New York, NY 10019) has available:

8.   The Double Day -- an examination of Latin American working women and their struggles against inequity , both in their workplaces and in their homes (53 minutes); and

9.   We Dig Coal -- an excellent, although somewhat dated, documentary about women coal miners (58 minutes).

From Women Make Movies (462 Broadway, Suite 500, New York, NY 10013):

10. Railroad Women -- an historical and contemporary look at women's work on U.S. railroads; profiles two women who work today in the railroad industry (30 minutes);

11. Women: The New Poor -- focuses on four women to explore the problem of the feminization of poverty (28 minutes);

12. Once This Land Was Ours -- portrays the struggle of female agricultural workers in India and the daily difficulties they confront in trying to provide for their families (19 minutes).

Other relevant films:

13. Fast Food Women -- provides a close-up look at the lives of women, mostly middle-aged with dependent children, who work in the fast food industry (28 minutes; Appalshop, 306FF Madison St., Whiteburg, KY 41858).

14. We Weren't Asking for the Moon -- a documentary from Mexico that depicts the difficulties that female garment workers in that country overcame in order to form a union and to recover from the devastating consequences of the 1985 earthquake in Mexico (58 minutes; First Run/Icarus Films, 153 Waverly Place, New York, NY 10014).

15. Good Monday Morning -- a powerful documentary about women office workers and various problems they confront on the job (30 minutes; available from: Fanlight Productions (47 Halifax Street, Boston, MA 02130).

Resources:

1. Among the many organizations that focus on sexism in the workplace are: The Institute for Women and Work, Cornell University, 15 East 26th Street, New York, NY 10010; the National Committee on Pay Equity, 1201 Sixteenth Street, NW, Suite 420, Washington, DC 20036; and 9 to 5, National Association of Working Women, 614 Superior Avenue, NW, Room 852, Cleveland, OH 44113.

2. For information on pensions, Social Security benefits, and other economic issues of special interest to older women, contact: the Older Women's League, 730 Eleventh Street, NW, Suite 300, Washington, DC 20001.

3. The Institute for Women's Policy Research (IWPR) conducts research, develops policy, and lobbies lawmakers on various gender-related work and economic issues, including poverty, welfare reform, health insurance coverage, and the glass ceiling. Contact IWPR at: 1400 20th St., NW, Suite 104, Washington, DC 20036.

See also: Sociologists Against Sexual Harassment (SASH) (Chapter 5).

CHAPTER NINE

Multiple Choice

1.   Until 1971, states could maintain that women were not legally
     'persons' based on which Supreme Court decision?
   * a.   In re Lockwood
     b.   In re Adler
     c.   Muller v. Oregon
     d.   Brown v. State of Virginia

2.   Traditionally, criminological research on women focused on:
     a.   their crime rates relative to those of men
     b.   low prostitution
     c.   the similarity between women's and men's crimes
     d.   the depravity of violent women
   * e.   all of the above, except c

3.   According to Freda Adler's study of the Uniform Crime Reports
     during the 1960s:
     a.   the male crime rate increased more than the female crime
          rate
   * b.   women were committing crimes that were traditionally
          committed only by men
     c.   men were committing more property crimes than women
     d.   none of the above

4.   Adler and Simon's argument that changes in the rate and character
     of female crime during the 1960s and 1970s were the logical out-
     comes of the women's liberation movement is known as:
     a.   the feminization of crime
     b.   the chivalry hypothesis
   * c.   emancipation theory
     d.   victimization theory

5.   One of the more accurate ways to measure changes in men's
     and women's respective criminal activity is:
     a.   to study only crimes known to the police
     b.   to look at how many crimes each sex commits annually
          and calculate for each the percentage increase or
          decrease from year to year
   * c.   to calculate sex-specific arrest rates (the number of
          arrests per 100,000 of the population) and then deter-
          mining the sex differential in arrests
     d.   none of the above

6.   Recent research indicates that the crime most frequently
     committed by women is:
     a.   murder
   * b.   larceny/theft
     c.   prostitution
     d.   arson

7. With respect to the relationship between drugs and criminal activity, research indicates that:
   a. involvement in both drugs and crime begin together, usually during adolescence
   b. the greater an individual's drug use, the more likely the individual is to be involved in other types of crime
   c. drug use can lead to greater criminal activity, but a lucrative criminal career can also promote drug use
   * d. all of the above

8. Inciardi and his colleagues have concluded from their research that the one way that crack cocaine relative to other drugs has a unique impact on women is:
   * a. the prevalence of the exchange of sex for the drug
   b. the different high that women get from the drug when compared with men
   c. the extent to which women more than men are willing to steal to obtain money to buy the drug
   d. the younger age at which women start using the drug

9. Women's white-collar criminal activity:
   a. is composed primarily of corporate crime
   b. could best be classified as typically serious rather than petty
   * c. tends to be motivated by family responsibilities rather than personal excess or corporate profit-making
   d. brings tremendous financial gain to the offenders involved

10. Which of the following explanations for the increase in female property crimes in recent years receives greatest support from research?
    a. technological innovations in the home have provided women with more opportunities to shoplift and perpetrate bad check passing
    b. worsening economic conditions of women have caused them to engage in property crimes
    * c. criminal justice personnel are more likely to apprehend and prosecute women
    d. historically crime rates did not accurately count the number of women committing petty crimes

11. Within police training academies and police departments:
    a. women are now regarded as the full equals of their male colleagues
    b. the behavior of women and men is evaluated using identical criteria so as to avoid sex discrimination
    * c. a belief in male superiority remains strong
    d. the workplace has been successfully "desexualized"

12. Evidence indicates that female police officers:
    a. differ significantly on most measures from their male
        colleagues in terms of attitudes toward police work
  * b. express greater job satisfaction than male officers do
    c. have higher self-confidence than male officers do
    d. are impeded in their job performance by low levels of
        self-confidence

13. Research indicates that female correctional officers:
    a. now experience little sex discrimination on the job
  * b. confront more resistance and harassment from male ad-
        ministrators and coworkers than from inmates
    c. differ from male correctional officers in their atti-
        tudes toward inmates
    d. express lower career commitment than male correctional
        officers do

14. Female attorneys:
    a. escape sexist prejudice and discrimination largely be-
        cause of the greater prestige attached to their pro-
        fession
    b. experience sex discrimination primarily in the lower
        courts, but rarely in the federal courts where affirma-
        tive action regulations are stricter
  * c. frequently are subjected to disparaging and offensive
        remarks and behaviors by colleagues and judges, both
        inside and outside the courtroom
    d. none of the above

15. With respect to plea bargaining:
    a. it is estimated that less than 50% of all criminal
        convictions are the result of negotiated guilty pleas
    b. research indicates that the poor and racial minorities
        are less likely than members of other groups to
        negotiate their pleas
    c. studies show that negotiated pleas result in stiffer
        sentences for offenders, regardless of sex or race
  * d. women appear to be less successful than men in nego-
        tiating sentence reductions despite the fact that they
        commit less serious crimes than men

16. With regard to female offenders, which of the following is
    most strongly related to sentence severity?
    a. prior record
    b. seriousness of crime
  * c. conformity to traditional norms of respectable femininity
    d. race

17. Research that examines the intersection of race and sex on
    sentencing and punishment shows that:
    * a.   minority women are more likely than white women to be
           sentenced to prison
      b.   minority women convicted of crimes against the person
           typically receive prison sentences almost twice as
           long as white women
      c.   the actual prison time served by white women is longer
           than the actual prison time served by minority women
      d.   all of the above

18. Which of the following is true regarding status offenses?
      a.   boys and girls are equally likely to be charged
      b.   boys are charged ten times more often than girls
      c.   by definition, only girls can be charged with a status
           offense
    * d.   girls are more frequently charged than boys

19. Of the following, who is likely to be sentenced most severe-
    ly?
      a.   a married, employed black man without a prior record
    * b.   an unmarried, unemployed white man with a record
      c.   an unmarried, unemployed black man without a prior record
      d.   none of the above because sentencing disparity has been
           eliminated by sentencing guidelines

20. Prison education and vocational training programs for women:
      a.   concentrate on equipping the inmates with salable
           skills
           to increase their prospects for employment once they
           are released from prison
      b.   are more numerous than those available to men
      c.   overemphasize the skilled trades
    * d.   typically train inmates for traditional female roles,
           such as clerical/office work, domestic work, and
           garment manufacturing

21. Among incarcerated women:
      a.   fewer than 40% are mothers of dependent children
    * b.   four out of five lived with their dependent children
           before they were imprisoned
      c.   those with dependent children typically rely on the
           children's father to care for the children during the
           period of incarceration
      d.   those with dependent children see these children on
           average three times a week during regular visitation
           periods
      e.   all of the above

22. Which of the following groups has the highest rate of vic-
    timization?
      a.   the elderly
      b.   young white women
    * c.   young men of color
      d.   young women of color

23. Hate crimes:
    a. officially cover all crimes in which the offender's actions are motivated by bias or hatred based on the victim's race, sex, sexual orientation or religion
    b. have decreased dramatically in recent years
  * c. involving gay and lesbian victims have been one of the fastest growing types of hate crimes in the U.S.
    d. typically result in less physical and psychological harm to victims than other types of assaults do

24. Studies indicate the crime that women, in general, fear most is:
    a. homicide
  * b. rape
    c. assault and battery
    d. robbery

25. All of the following is true about rape EXCEPT:
    a. 1 out of 12 women will be a victim of rape or attempted rape in her lifetime
    b. victims must prove their innocence to the court rather than the state proving the guilt of the rapist
  * c. studies show that the fastest growing type of rape involves homosexual men and young children
    d. it is commonly believed that most women precipitate the assault

26. The majority of rapes are:
  * a. acquaintance rapes
    b. reported to the police
    c. committed by strangers
    d. perpetrated when women go out alone at night

27. Charges of marital rape:
    a. rarely occur in the United States
  * b. have a high conviction rate, if the cases go to trial
    c. occur when one person gives in to his/her spouse to please them
    d. when investigated, are frequently dismissed as untrue

28. It is estimated that _____ percent of ever-married women have been raped by their husbands.
    a. 2
  * b. 12
    c. 25
    d. 50

29. According to the authors of your textbook, which of the
    following is the best explanation for the high rate of rape
    in the U.S.?
    a.   there is an unequal power relationship between men and women
    b.   violence against women is condoned in this society
    c.   the mentally disturbed do not receive the medical attention
          that they so desperately need
  * d.   both a and b above

30. Men's exposure to violent pornography:
    a.   increases their sensitivity to rape
  * b.   increases their self reported possibility of raping
    c.   decreases men's likelihood of raping
    d.   has no impact on men's attitudes toward rape

31. The Meese Commission (1986) found which of the following
    forms of pornographic material to increase persons' accept-
    ance of rape myths?
    a.   nonviolent material that depict degradation
    b.   nonviolent and nondegrading material
    c.   violent material
    d.   all of the above
  * e.   both a and c above

True/False:

32. In the United States, criminal law is created to best repre-
    sent the interests of all segments of society equally.
    a.   true
  * b.   false

33. The FBI's Uniform Crime Reports accurately reflect actual
    rates of criminal behavior in the United States.
    a.   true
  * b.   false

34. Most female offenders are committing what are considered
    traditional crimes for members of their sex.
  * a.   true
    b.   false

35. Sentencing disparity is frequently the result of extra-legal
    factors such as sex and race.
  * a.   true
    b.   false

36. Prostitutes are generally left alone by the criminal justice
    system because they are involved in "the world's oldest
    profession".
    a.   true
  * b.   false

37. Victims of hate-motivated assaults typically suffer greater
    physical and psychological harm than victims of other
    assaults.
    * a.   true
      b.   false

38. Rape has one of the lowest conviction rates of any type of
    crime.
    * a.   true
      b.   false

39. Acquaintance rape comprises one half of all reported incid-
    ents of sexual assault.
    * a.   true
      b.   false

40. The younger the rape victim, the less likely she is to know
    her assailant.
      a.   true
    * b.   false

41. Almost half of all rapes take place at or in the victim's
    home or the home of one of the victim's friends, relatives
    or neighbors.
    * a.   true
      b.   false

42. Race of the offender is an important element in sentencing
    severity in rape cases.
    * a.   true
      b.   false

43. Historically, federal commissioned reports on pornography
    have shown consistently that pornography is causally related
    to sexual violence against women.
      a.   true
    * b.   false

44. Violence against women is considered a human rights problem
    by most governments throughout the world today.
      a.   true
    * b.   false

Essays:

45. Discuss three ways in which the criminal justice system in
    the United States reinforces gender inequality.

46. What is sentencing disparity and how is it related to tradi-
    tional gender stereotypes? Be sure to include a reference
    to status offenses.

47. It has been argued that women's criminal victimization is
    often rendered invisible. Explain this position.

48. Identify three specific rape myths and discuss research evidence that refutes each one.

49. Should specific forms of violence against women be officially labeled "hate crimes"? Why or why not?

50. What is the relationship between pornography and violence against women?

51. Many forms of institutionalized violence against women, such as female circumcision, are perpetrated by women themselves. How can this apparent paradox be explained?

Classroom Activities/Take-home Assignments:

1.   If your college or university is located in an area where there is access to both a female and a male detention facility, it may be instructive to arrange for students to visit these institutions and to compare the facilities and programs in each. It would also be instructive for students to have the opportunity to meet with at least a small group of inmates at the respective institutions and to get a sense of the differences in the offenses for which they have been imprisoned as well as their different concerns and backgrounds. Students, however, must be well-prepared by the instructor before they make such visits.

2.   Ask your students to research the rape laws of your state and to identify the sexist (and homophobic) stereotypes that underlie these.

Film Suggestions:

1.   Blind Justice: Women and the Law -- four animated segments that trace the ways that justice has been applied to women historically and in contemporary societies; includes a segment on the negative impact of detention on young girls who are institutionalized "for their own good" (30 minutes; available from: Films for the Humanities and Sciences, P.O. Box 2053, Princeton, NJ 08543).

2.   Girltalk -- focuses on three teenage girls who are runaways and shows their survival strategies (58 minutes; available from: Filmakers Library, 124 East 40th St., New York, NY 10016).

3.   Locking Up Women -- focuses on changes at Holloway, a women's prison in Britain which, at one time, was a dreaded women's institution because of its lock-down philosophy, but which has changed in recent years; this film is less impressive in its consideration of the question of how women's criminal activity has changed in recent years and its emphasis on the psychological

underpinnings of women's criminal activity (52 minutes; available from: Films for the Humanities and Sciences, P.O. Box 2053, Princeton, NJ 08543).

4. They're Doing My Time -- an award-winning documentary on incarcerated mothers, highlighting the plight of their children, but also examining programs in prisons and jails that are attempting to address the problem (56 minutes; available from: The Cinema Guild, 1697 Broadway, New York, NY 10019).

There are several excellent films available on sexual assault and related issues. Among them are:

5. Rape/Crisis -- a docudrama that investigates the trauma of rape by focusing on the crisis for all involved, the interrogation of suspects, and the work of a rape crisis center (87 minutes; available from: The Cinema Guild, 1697 Broadway, New York, NY 10019);

6. Rape: Face to Face -- explores the causes and consequences of rape and includes an emotional confrontation between convicted rapists and women who have been raped though not by these men (55 minutes; available from: The Filmmakers Library, 124 East 40th Street, New York, NY 10016);

7. An Ordinary Rape -- debunks the myths surrounding date rape; includes interviews with high school and college students, criminologists, psychologists, and others (54 minutes; available from: First Run/Icarus Films, 153 Waverly Place, New York, NY 10014);

8. Rape by Any Name -- also focuses on date and acquaintance rape, exploring the topic through interviews with survivors, college students, and counselors (60 minutes; available from: Women Make Movies, 462 Broadway, Suite 500, New York, NY 10013);

9. Dating Rites: Gang Rape on Campus -- a documentary on gang rape as well as date rape on college and university campuses in the United States; includes an eight-minute segment that illustrates how a gang rape is planned (28 minutes; available from: Filmakers Library, 124 East 40th St., New York, NY 10016);

10. Two Accused: Chronicle of a Rape Trial -- uses a hypothetical high-profile rape case to explore issues such as media coverage of rape trials and related issues; panelists include Supreme Court Justice Antonin Scalia and journalist Anna Quindlen (60 minutes; available from: PBS Video, 1320 Braddock Place, Alexandria, VA 22314); and

11. Rape Culture -- examines portrayals of rape in film, advertising, songs, and other media, and emphasizes the relationship between sexual violence and what is considered "normal" male-female interaction in our society.

Three films on pornography are:

12. Not a Love Story: A Film About Pornography -- a controversial documentary that vividly presents the case against pornography. Students should be forewarned of the film's sexually explicit content (69 minutes; available from: National Film Board of Canada, 1251 Avenue of the Americas, 16th Floor, New York, NY 10020);

13. Pornography: The Double Message -- a video that in 1987 won an award from the American Psychological Association, explores the effects that hard-core pornography may have on our society, including consideration of whether it desensitizes people to violence. It surveys extensively the available research on the effects of violent pornography (28 minutes; available from: Filmmakers Library, 124 East 40th St., New York, NY 10016); and

14. Patently Offensive: Porn Under Siege -- provides a careful examination of all sides of the pornography debate and includes exclusive footage of the Meese Commission hearings (58 minutes; available from: Filmakers Library, 124 East 40th St., New York, NY 10016).

Several outstanding films are available that focus on hate violence against women, institutionalized violence against women, and human rights issues. Among them are:

15. Just Because of Who We Are -- a documentary that examines the problem of hate-motivated violence against lesbians (28 minutes; available from: Women Make Movies, 462 Broadway, Suite 500, New York, NY 10013);

16. After the Montreal Massacre -- examines the shooting of fourteen women at the University of Montreal in 1989 by placing the incident in the context of other kinds of violence against women; includes interviews with a survivor and other students as well as activists and journalists (27 minutes; Women Make Movies, 462 Broadway, Suite 500, New York, NY 10013);

17. Warrior Marks -- produced by Alice Walker and directed by Pratibha Parmar, this film examines the problem of female genital mutilation in Africa and includes interviews with African women as well as women in the United States and England interspersed with Walker's reflections on the practice (54 minutes; Women Make Movies, 462 Broadway, Suite 500, New York, NY 10013);

18. Rites -- also sensitively explores the custom of female circumcision and considers three major contexts in which it occurs (52 minutes; available from: Filmakers Library, 124 East 40th St., New York, NY 10016);

19. Senso Daughters -- an historical documentary that chronicles the experiences of Japanese and Korean women who were brought to Papua New Guinea during World War II when the Japanese occupied that country. The were used as "comfort women" (military prosti-

tutes) for Japanese troops; includes interviews with survivors (54 minutes; available from: First Run/Icarus Films, 153 Waverly Place, New York, NY 10014); and

20. Dance of Hope -- focuses on human rights in Chile and the women there who have become activists in response to the detention and disappearance of their loved ones (75 minutes; available from: First Run/Icarus Films, 153 Waverly Place, New York, NY 10014).

See also: Rate It X (Chapter 1)

Resources:

1. The Women and Crime Division of the American Society of Criminology publishes a newsletter and also has available a set of curriculum materials on gender, crime, and justice. Contact: American Society of Criminology, Women and Crime Division, 1314 Kinnear Road, Suite 212, Columbus, OH 43212.

2. The National Women's Law Center (1616 P St., Suite 100, Washington, DC) provides technical assistance and lobbies on behalf of women with respect to all aspects of the law.

3. FEMJUR is a feminist jurisprudence email forum devoted to the discussion of theories and issues related to feminism, women and the law. To subscribe:

Send this message: SUBSCRIBE FEMJUR <YOUR NAME> (your real name, not your email id)

to: LISTSERV@SUVM (bitnet) or: LISTSERV@SUVM.SYR.EDU (internet); leave the subject line blank

4. There are several organizations that offer resources on hate crimes and hate-motivated violence. The include: the Center for the Advanced Study of Prejudice and Ethnoviolence, 31 S. Greene St., Baltimore, MD 21201; the New York City Gay and Lesbian Anti-Violence Project, 647 Hudson, New York, NY 10014; and Community United Against Violence, 973 Market St., San Francisco, CA 94103. The Center for Women Policy Studies (2000 P St., NW, Suite 508, Washington, DC 20036) also has available an excellent position paper on violence against women as hate crimes.

5. For information on sexual assault, rape prevention, rape crisis counseling, and related issues, contact: The National Coalition Against Sexual Assault, The Sexual Violence Center, 1222 West 31st Street, Minneapolis, MN 55408, OR your local rape crisis center.

There also is an electronic forum for sexual assault activists. To subscribe:

Send this message: SUBSCRIBE STOPRAPE <YOUR NAME> (your real name, not your email id)

to: LISTSERVE@BROWNVM (bitnet) or: LISTSERV@BROWNV.BROWN.EDU (internet); leave the subject line blank.

6.   Resources with respect to violence against women as a human rights issues include:

Publications from the Center for Women's Global Leadership, 27 Clifton Ave., Douglass College, Rutgers University, New Brunswick, NJ 08903.

The Violence Against Women Program at the MATCH International Centre, 1102-200 Elgin St., Ottawa, Ontario, Canada K2P 1L5.

A 354-page report available from the United Nations Development Fund for Women (UNIFEM) which addresses women's efforts throughout the world to combat violence. The report is entitled, "Free From Violence: Women's Strategies from Around the World."

The International Women's Rights Action Watch (Humphrey Institute of Public Affairs, University of Minnesota, 301 19th Avenue South, Minneapolis, MN 55455) has a bibliography available entitled, "Women's International Human Rights: A Bibliography."

Human Rights Watch (485 Fifth Ave., New York, NY 10017) has a Women's Rights Project through which they monitor various types of human rights violations, such as sexual slavery.

Amnesty International has available a report on human rights violations against women entitled, "Women In the Front Lines" (1991). To obtain a copy of the report ($6.00 + $1.75 postage/handling) and for further information on political prisoners and prisoners of conscience, contact: Amnesty International, 322 Eighth Avenue, New York, NY 10001.

See also: The National Clearinghouse for the Defense of Battered Women (Chapter 7), and the Family Violence and Sexual Assault Institute (Chapter 7)

CHAPTER TEN

Multiple Choice:

1. The Presidential election of _____ was important because it was
    the first time that the women's vote was significantly different
    from the men's vote.
    a.   1920
    * b.   1980
    c.   1976
    d.   1952

2. A strong and consistent gender gap in political attitudes
    emerges with respect to all of the following EXCEPT:
    a.   economic issues
    b.   energy issues
    c.   social welfare issues
    * d.   issues of war and peace

3. Research on voters' preferences indicates that women voters are
    more likely than male voters to:
    a.   favor construction of more nuclear power plants
    b.   disapprove of increased spending on job training programs
    c.   support U.S. troops invading another country
    * d.   support increased government spending on social
         programs

4. Social science research indicates that:
    a.   women vote for candidates based on their looks or
         style
    b.   women are more conservative than male voters
    c.   husbands strongly influence their wives' voting
         patterns
    * d.   none of the above

5. Research on political activism indicates that women are more
    likely than men to engage in:
    a.   party conventions
    b.   transitional activities
    * c.   spectator activities
    d.   gladiator activities

6. Women are almost twice as likely as men:
    * a.   to work on a political campaign
    b.   to be a delegate to a major party's convention
    c.   to make a monetary campaign contribution
    d.   to run for political office

7. Women are less likely than men to run for public office because:
   a. they lack the necessary skills and knowledge
   b. they feel they are needed in the home which is their primary responsibility
 * c. they face prejudice and discrimination both among the electorate and within party organizations
   d. they have been socialized not to develop the qualities needed to be successful politicians

8. Female candidates for political office:
   a. typically are perceived by the electorate as similar to male candidates
   b. are viewed by the electorate as more knowledgeable on foreign policy issues than male candidates are
   c. usually are considered by the electorate as being more capable of managing large budgets than male candidates are
 * d. are perceived by the electorate as being better than male candidates at handling education issues

9. Recent research on media coverage of political candidates indicates that:
   a. female candidates receive more coverage than male candidates if a campaign is especially competitive
   b. female candidates receive more coverage than male candidates if the women are incumbents rather than challengers
 * c. coverage of female candidates tends to focus on their chances of winning, whereas coverage of male candidates focuses more on campaign issues
   d. female candidates receive more coverage of their positions on national security, whereas male candidates receive more coverage of their positions on domestic spending

10. The most formidable obstacle for female candidates seeking to win a political office is:
    a. discrimination against them within political parties
 * b. incumbency
    c. media coverage of their campaigns
    d. lack of experience in policy-making positions

11. Campaign fundraising may be difficult for female and minority candidates because:
    a. they have less experience than male candidates in managing large budgets
    b. they fail to seek assistance from Political Action Committees which play a major role in campaign financing
 * c. the constituencies they represent may have little discretionary income
    d. all of the above

12. Women as office holders have made the greatest gains in which political category?
    * a. state government
    b. local government
    c. federal government
    d. there has been no significant gains made anywhere

13. Of the following, which is true with regard to "widow's succession"?
    a. it occurs when a congressman dies or becomes ill and his wife is appointed to finish his term
    b. it was the primary means to the office of Senator for women until the 1980s
    c. it was abolished in 1977
    d. all of the above
    * e. both a and b above

14. It was not until the elections of _____ that women and minorities made significant progress in Congressional officeholding.
    a. 1965
    b. 1980
    c. 1984
    * d. 1992

15. It is especially important for the President to name women and minorities for federal appointed positions because:
    a. such appointments set an example for private employers to follow in hiring personnel
    b. such positions provide young professional women and minorities with valuable career experience
    c. such positions offer opportunities for input into policy making from individuals with diverse backgrounds and interests
    * d. all of the above

16. According to the 1948 Women's Armed Services Integration Act:
    a. women were required to compose 25% of the armed forces
    b. female officers were restricted from wearing make-up
    * c. women were restricted from becoming generals or admirals
    d. women were entitled to learn hand-to-hand combat

17. In the late 1960's and early 1970's, a series of events took place that expanded both the number and roles of women in the armed forces. Which of the following is not such an event?
    * a. Grove City College v Bell
    b. Frontiero v Richardson
    c. Public Law 90-30
    d. creation of the all-volunteer Force

18. In the 1980's:
    a.   the number of minority women in the military decreased
  * b.   the number of minority women in the military increased
    c.   there were more black officers than white officers
    d.   the number of Hispanic officers rose dramatically

19. The risk rule:
    a.   was utilized by the U.S. military until 1994
    b.   determined the military jobs from which women would be
         barred
    c.   referred to the military's policy of excluding women
         from ground combat and combat support positions that
         entailed a substantial risk of being killed in action
         or being taken as a prisoner of war
  * d.   all of the above

20. All of the following are true with regard to women in the
    U.S. Armed Forces today EXCEPT:
    a.   women experience much sexual harassment
  * b.   women are restricted from flying military aircraft
    c.   women on average are paid a lower salary than men
    d.   women are prohibited from holding positions that have a
         high probability of fighting enemy forces in close
         combat under hostile fire at or near front lines

21. The current federal policy with regard to gays and lesbians
    in the U.S. military:
    a.   is considered by most observers to be significantly
         more progressive than the previous policy, directive
         No. 1332.4
    b.   reflects the general public's overwhelming support
         for a total ban on gays and lesbians in the military
  * c.   allows gays and lesbians to serve in the military as
         long as they are not open about their sexual orienta-
         tion and do not engage in homosexual acts
    d.   prohibits gays and lesbians from serving in any branch
         of the armed forces

True/False:

22. The ratification of the Constitution of the United States
    resulted in a loss of rights for women.
  * a.   true
    b.   false

23. Numerically, women compose a larger percentage of the voting
    population than men.
  * a.   true
    b.   false

24. Black women have increased their voting rate faster than
    black men.
  * a.   true
    b.   false

25. Minority women tend to vote similarly to white women in political elections.
   a.   true
 * b.   false

26. Men are more interested in politics than women are.
   a.   true
 * b.   false

27. In recent years, the Republican party has adopted programs that have dramatically increased the percentage of female representation at their political conventions.
   a.   true
 * b.   false

28. Female officeholders are more likely than their male counterparts to have held previous appointed government positions before running for office themselves.
 * a.   true
   b.   false

29. Historical studies reveal that women have rarely played a vital role in the military activities of the U.S.
   a.   true
 * b.   false

30. Women may now legally hold combat-support roles in the Armed Forces.
 * a.   true
   b.   false

31. The U.S. Armed Forces is the most "equal opportunity employer" that exists.
   a.   true
 * b.   false

Essays:

32. The gender gap in political attitudes and voting is complex. A number of other variables intersect with sex to influence attitudes and voting. Explain.

33. Why are women so scarce in political offices? Give some explanations for this and offer some possible solutions.

34. Discuss women's roles in state and federal government. Address the differences between minority and white women's experiences.

35. Discuss the problems of sexual harassment and harassment of homosexuals in the military. What accounts for the pervasiveness of these problems in the armed forces?

36. Discuss the problems that gay and lesbian military personnel currently confront. Does the research evidence support or refute the exclusion of homosexuals from the military?

3. Why is gender inequality in politics and the military important to gender inequality in society as a whole? What can be done to alter prevalent conditions of discrimination?

Classroom Activity/Take-home Assignment:

Ask your students to trace the history of the election of women and minorities to public office in your state or local government. If there is an upcoming election in your area, students would also find it instructive to observe differences in men's and women's voting patterns, and in minorities' voting patterns. Are there differences in the way the media cover female versus male candidates? Or, on referendum issues, ask them to determine if there was a gender gap, race gap, sexual orientation gap, and/or age gap in voting and to account for these various differences.

Film Suggestions:

1. Women's Voices: The Gender Gap Movie -- a brief, entertaining look at the gender gap which takes three approaches: interviews with 15 women from diverse backgrounds; statistics about the gender gap; and animated footage of Sylvia, Nicole Hollander's cartoon character (16 minutes; available from: New Day Films, 853 Broadway, Suite 1210, New York, NY 10003).

Also available from New Day Films:

2. Metropolitan Avenue -- shows women's grassroots political activism in the moving account of community organizing in a Brooklyn, NY neighborhood (49 minutes).

Other films about gender and politics include:

3. Women in Politics -- looks at the increasing number of women running for and being elected to political office; explores the challenges these candidates face in the political arena (60 minutes; available from: PBS Video, 1320 Braddock Place, Alexandria, VA 22314);

4. Wilma P. Mankiller: Woman of Power -- profiles the first female chief of the Cherokee Nation in the United States (29 minutes; available from: Women Make Movies, 462 Broadway, Suite 500, New York, NY 10013;

5. Jeannette Rankin: The Woman Who Voted No -- Jeannette Rankin was the first woman elected to national office in the United States. Elected to the U.S. Congress in 1916, she voted against

U.S. involvement in both world wars, decisions that eventually ended her political career. This film chronicles that career (30 minutes; available from: PBS Video, 1320 Braddock Place, Alexandria, VA 22314); and

6.   Clarence Thomas and Anita Hill: Public Hearing, Private Pain -- a segment of the "Frontline" series, this video focuses on the racial aspects of the Thomas nomination and confirmation hearings as well as the gender issues involved; shows how race was used to divide particular groups, including the black community itself (60 minutes; available from: PBS Video, 1320 Braddock Place, Alexandria, VA 22314).

Films that examine gender issues in the military and warfare include three excellent films from Filmakers Library (124 East 40th St., New York, NY 10016):

7.   Comrades in Arms -- gay men and lesbians who served with honor in the British armed forces during World War II recall how they had to hide their sexual orientation and carry on secret lives because of the military's ban on homosexuals (52 minutes);

8.   Burden of War -- addresses the usually overlooked fact that women who served in Vietnam, like men, were exposed to Agent Orange and currently are experiencing, along with their children, its devastating effects (30 minutes); and

9.   Women in War: Voices from the Front Lines -- an insightful examination of the effects of war and the efforts of women in various countries in the world (e.g., Northern Ireland, El Salvador) to bring about peace (48 minutes).

Available from Women Make Movies (462 Broadway, Suite 500, New York, NY 10013):

10.   As the Mirror Burns -- a documentary about Vietnamese women who served in guerrilla forces during the Vietnam War; shows how the war continues to impact on the lives of women in Vietnam (58 minutes); and

11.   Algeria: Women at War -- shows the central role Algerian women played in their country's struggle to gain independence from France; looks at the conditions under which contemporary Algerian women live and raises the question of whether it is possible to strike a balance between the struggle for women's liberation and the struggle for national liberation (52 minutes).

We also highly recommend:

12.   Through the Wire -- a frightening political documentary about a controversial high security unit of the federal prison in Lexington, KY, opened in 1986. Its only inmates were three women serving long sentences for nonviolent, politically-motivated crimes. The film documents the inhumane treatment to which the women were subjected and reviews a federal lawsuit on their

behalf. Although the initial federal court hearing did find on behalf of the women, this ruling was overturned on appeal in 1989. Sixteen new units modeled after this one are now being built. This is a moving and shocking film (68 minutes; available from: the Cinema Guild, 1697 Broadway, New York, NY 10019).

Resources:

1.   In addition to the resources listed in the text, an excellent source of information on gender-related political issues is: the National Women's Political Caucus, 1275 K Street, NW, Suite 750, Washington, DC 20005. Besides keeping track of election results and political appointments, NWPC holds periodic conferences and workshops, often providing assistance to women who wish to become more active in politics.

2.   The Gay and Lesbian Caucus for Political Science may be contacted c/o Len Hirsch, 1442 Q St., NW, Washington, DC 20009-3808.

3.   An electronic forum for the discussion of feminism, gender, women and international relations is available. To subscribe:

        Send this message: SUBSCRIBE FEMISA <YOUR NAME> (remember that this refers to your real name and not your email id)

        to: LISTSERV@CSF.COLORADO.EDU (internet); leave the subject line blank.

4.   Various resources on gender and the military, gender and warfare, and gender and peace are available from the following organizations:

Women Against Intervention/War, 3411, W. Diversey St., Chicago, IL 60647;

Women's Actions for New Directions, P.O. Box B, Arlington, MA 02174;

Women Strike for Peace, 110 Maryland Ave., NE, #302, Washington, DC 20002; and

Women's International League for Peace and Freedom, 1213 Race St., Philadelphia, PA 19107.

CHAPTER ELEVEN

Multiple Choice:

1. Religion is very appealing because:
    a. it gives meaning to human existence
    b. it provides its followers with a sense of belonging
    c. it lends order to social life by establishing behavioral
        standards
  * d. all of the above

2. The intensity of commitment of an individual or group to a
    religious belief system is called:
    a. spirituality
  * b. religiosity
    c. piety
    d. religious universality

3. The largest number of persons claiming to have no religious
    identification is:
    a. women
    b. Hispanics
  * c. men
    d. blacks

4. In ancient goddess worshiping societies:
    a. motherhood was frequently devalued
    b. female gods were ascribed only feminine traits
  * c. female gods were believed to be more powerful than male gods
    d. male gods did not exist

5. Patriarchal religions supplanted matriarchal ones when:
    a. the role of males in the reproductive process became better
        understood
    b. the practice of witchcraft became popular
    c. political battles were fought and matriarchal societies lost
        because they were pacifistic
  * d. both a and c are possible explanations

6. In its earliest days, witchcraft:
    a. was condemned by Christianity
    b. was participated in by both men and women
    c. was associated with devil worship
  * d. peacefully coexisted with established Christianity

7. Orthodox Judaism:
    a. maintains that only men can acquire property
  * b. maintains that divorce is unilateral
    c. promotes the participation of women in religious study
    d. maintains that men and women have the same religious
        obligations

8. In which of the following areas may it be argued that Orthodox Judaism does not have repressive policies towards women?
    a. marriage
  * b. sexual fulfillment in marriage
    c. divorce
    d. practicing religion

9. The laws of Orthodox Judaism emphasize:
    a. "the physical and spiritual togetherness of the sexes"
  * b. "the physical and spiritual apartness of the sexes"
    c. "the holiness and superiority of women"
    d. none of the above

10. Kaufman's study of newly Orthodox Jewish women indicates that:
  * a. these women value the family purity laws and other halakic prescriptions in part because such rituals give them control of their sexuality
    b. most of these women identify themselves as feminists
    c. the majority of these women regret their decision to convert to Orthodoxy because they find it far too repressive
    d. these women tend to feel diminished in status relative to their Orthodox husbands

11. The Reform movement of Judaism:
    a. abolished the seating division of men and women in the synagogue
    b. admitted women to the rabbinical seminary
    c. established educational organizations for women
  * d. all of the above

12. Which of the following congregations has the largest number of female rabbis?
    a. Orthodox Judaism
  * b. Reform Judaism
    c. Conservative Judaism
    d. women are never allowed to be rabbis

13. Historically Christianity has characterized women in all of the following ways EXCEPT as:
    a. evil temptress
    b. good mother
    c. virginal
  * d. Christ-like

14. The Catholic church is opposed to:
    a. the ordination of women
    b. artificial contraception
    c. homosexuality
  * d. all of the above

15. Research on Protestant churches indicates that:
   * a.   the number of women entering divinity schools and seminaries
         is increasing
    b.   the number of women entering divinity schools and seminaries
         is decreasing
    c.   sexism is not prevalent within Protestant churches
    d.   female clergy members are paid the same as male clergy
         members

16. According to the history of Islam, the prophet Mohammed decreed
    that:
    a.   men and women were created equal, and should thus be treated
         accordingly
    b.   the care of children was exclusively the job of women
   * c.   men were the official "guardians" of women
    d.   women should be afforded multiple husbands to increase their
         likelihood of having many children

17. The current teachings of Islam:
    a.   maintain that members of the opposite sex should be united
         in everything they do
    b.   promote the equality of women
   * c.   maintain that members of the opposite sex should be kept
         separate
    d.   promote the equality of women only in terms of religious
         participation

18. Traditionally, minority churches have been:
    a.   as conservative as the "New Right"
   * b.   centers for political and social activism
    c.   the only places that accept women of color as men's social
         equals
    d.   largely ignored by larger society

19. As a religious movement, feminist spirituality:
    a.   has abandoned Judeo-Christian religions
    b.   advocates a formal break with all that is male-oriented
   * c.   rejects the dualism of patriarchal religion
    d.   disregards homosexual and minority experiences

20. Feminist "reformers" are restructuring religious rituals in
    all of the following ways EXCEPT:
    a.   divesting God of masculine qualities
    b.   forming women's services and ceremonies
    c.   rediscovering Jesus' female disciples
   * d.   making religion only relevant for women

True/False:

21. Religion is a cultural universal.
   * a.   true
    b.   false

22. Historically and cross-culturally, God has always been por-
    trayed as masculine.
    a.   true
  * b.   false

23. More women than men conceptualize God as Mother.
  * a.   true
    b.   false

24. From the 15th to 18th centuries, Catholic and Protestant
    authorities killed between one million and nine million
    people accused of practicing witchcraft.
  * a.   true
    b.   false

25. According to Orthodox Jewish customs, women are "legally
    impure" for two weeks of every month.
  * a.   true
    b.   false

26. There is considerable evidence that leadership of the early
    Christian movement was shared by women and men.
  * a.   true
    b.   false

27. Surveys indicate that the majority of Catholics are satis-
    fied with the treatment women receive by the church.
    a.   true
  * b.   false

28. There are no Christian churches that permit the ordination
    of homosexuals as clergy.
    a.   true
  * b.   false

29. Islamic women have been given significantly greater freedom
    in terms of dress and mobility in most Muslim countries
    during the last decade.
    a.   true
  * b.   false

30. Research indicates that the majority of Islamic women
    have strongly resisted wearing the chador and adhering to
    the restrictions of purdah.
    a.   true
  * b.   false

Essays:

31. Use evidence from this chapter to refute the statement: God
    has been and always will be male.

32. Discuss Judaism and the role of Jewish women in this religious tradition. Cite specific differences among the three major Jewish congregations?

33. How does Christianity legitimize the role of women in the church as "second class citizens"? What can be done to change this?

34. What is the "stained glass ceiling"? Present evidence to either support or refute its existence.

35. Compare and contrast the religious traditions of Islam, Judaism, and Christianity with regard to the issues of women's role each religion.

36. The authors of your text discuss studies of women to have converted to religious orthodoxy. Discuss the findings of this research in terms of why orthodoxy might be especially appealing to women.

37. What is "feminist spirituality" and why is it important to changing the role of women in religion? In what ways would feminist spirituality come into conflict with the "New Right"?

38. What is ecofeminism? Why is this feminist perspective generating controversy among feminists?

Classroom Activity/Take-home Assignment:

Ask your students if they think God is male or female? Some will answer "male," but from our experience in gender courses, most students answer "neither." Ask them if they ever refer to their God as She? How often have they seen God depicted as female in prayer books or other religious books? The fact of the matter is that regardless of how much we may claim that God is sexless, we have learned to speak of God and to image God as male--as a scary old white male with a long white beard, to be more exact. To further sensitize students to the patriarchal nature of traditional religions, ask them to recite the following prayers, but as they do, they should change each masculine noun or pronoun to a feminine one (e.g., Father to Mother, Lord, to Lady):

> The angel of the Lord encamps around those who fear him, and delivers them. Taste and see how good the Lord is; happy the man who takes refuge in him.

> God, we praise you; Father all-powerful, Christ Lord and Savior, Spirit of love. Father of everlasting goodness, our origin and guide, be close to us and hear the prayers of all who praise you.

Discuss with the students how it makes them feel to pray to a
female deity and why they may feel that way. Ask them to review
these prayers once again, but this time they should make the
language gender-neutral. What are their reactions to praying to
a gender-neutral deity? What other language transformations can
they make to either de-gender or multi-engender prayer and religious ritual?

A variation on this exercise is to ask students to locate prayers
from their own religious traditions (if they have one) and to
transform the language as specified above.

Film Suggestions:

1.   A Lesbian in the Pulpit -- chronicles the struggle of Sally
Boyle, an ordained minister, and her partner to live as they are:
a loving, out lesbian couple; considers the position of the
United Church of Canada on issue of homosexuality as well as the
views of others, including relatives of the two women (28
minutes; available from: Filmakers Library, 124 East 40th St.,
New York, NY 10016).

2.   No Need to Repent: The Ballad of Rev. Jan Griesinger --
chronicles the life and ministry of the Rev. Jan Griesinger, an
ordained minister in the United Church of Christ and an out
lesbian; examines current debates in the church about women's
roles and about homosexuality (27 minutes; available from: Women
Make Movies, 462 Broadway, Suite 500, New York, NY 10013).

3.   Hidden Faces -- a documentary about the lives of Egyptian
women in their Muslim society (52 minutes; available from: Women
Make Movies, 462 Broadway, Suite 500, New York, NY 10013).

4.   The Women Next Door -- a documentary about women in the
Palestinian-Israeli conflict; shows the impact of this long
conflict on women on both sides (80 minutes; available from:
Women Make Movies, 462 Broadway, Suite 500, New York, NY 10013).

5.   Saints and Spirits -- shows three religious events in Moroc-
co, including pilgrimages to the shrines of Muslim saints (26
minutes; available from: First Run/Icarus Films, 153 Waverly
Place, New York, NY 10014).

6.   Who Will Cast the First Stone? -- an examination of the
impact of Islamization on women in Pakistan and the struggle of
some Pakistani women against the gender inequality that results
from it (52 minutes; available from: The Cinema Guild, 1697
Broadway, New York, NY 10019).

7.   The Religious Right -- an inside look at the "National
Affairs Briefing," a meeting of conservative evangelicals, during
which the "enemies" were clearly identified as homosexuals,
feminists, "abortionists," and the "secular media" (60 minutes;

available from: PBS Video, 1320 Braddock Place, Alexandria, VA 22314).

8.   Holy Terror -- an award-winning documentary that examines the activities of the religious New Right, in particular their anti- abortion activism and their impact on politics (58 minutes; available from: The Cinema Guild, 1697 Broadway, New York, NY 10019).

Resources:

1.   Task Force on Equality of Women In Judaism (838 Fifth Avenue, New York, NY 10021) provides information on religious equality for women in reform Judaism.

2.   Priests for Equality (P.O. Box 5243, West Hyattsville, MD 20782) has a number of informative pamphlets, reports, and research papers available on gender equality in the Catholic Church. Especially informative are their papers on the ordination of women.

3.   The National Council of Churches (475 Riverside Drive, New York, NY 10115) offers a number of publications on women and ministry, including pay equity issues and seminary/theological school enrollments.

There also are several electronic forums of interest:

     a.   FEMREL-L: focuses on women, religion and feminist theology; to subscribe:

     Send the message: SUBSCRIBE FEMREL-L <YOUR NAME>

     to: LISTSERV@MIZZOU1 (bitnet) or: LISTSERV@MIZZOU1.MISSOURI.EDU (internet); leave the subject line blank.

     b.   WMSPRT-L: focuses on women's spirituality and feminist religions; to subscribe:

     Send the message: SUBSCRIBE WMSPRT-L <YOUR NAME>

     to: LISTSERV@UBVM (bitnet) or: LISTSERV@UBVM.CC.BUFFALO.EDU (internet); leave the subject line blank.

     c.   BRIDGES: a Jewish feminist electronic forum; to subscribe:

     Send the message: SUBSCRIBE BRIDGES <YOUR NAME>.

     to: LISTSERV@ISRAEL.NYSERNET.ORG (internet); leave the subject line blank.

d.   SISTER-L: a forum for Catholic women religious, but also open to scholars, practitioners, and all other who share the concerns of nuns or religious sisters; to subscribe:

Send the message: SUBSCRIBE SISTER-L <YOUR NAME>

to: LISTSERV@SUVM.SYR.EDU (internet); leave the subject line blank.

CHAPTER TWELVE

Multiple Choice

1. Which of the following groups of people has the highest mortality
   rate?
   a.   white men
 * b.   black men
   c.   white women
   d.   black women

2. Women employed outside the home:
   a.   have higher rates of heart disease than full-time homemakers
   b.   have higher rates of heart disease than employed men
 * c.   appear to be healthier than nonemployed women
   d.   none of the above

3. In Third World countries:
   a.   life expectancy is quickly becoming equal to life ex-
        pectancy in economically developed countries
   b.   the gap between male and female life expectancies is
        wider than in industrialized countries
   c.   the gender gap in life expectancies is about 7 years
        in favor of women
 * d.   the sex difference in life expectancy is sometimes the
        reverse of that in industrialized countries

4. African Americans' higher rate of coronary heart disease
   appears to be related to:
 * a.   suppressed anger over racism
   b.   higher employment rates of women
   c.   an overuse of health care services
   d.   none of the above; African Americans do not have higher
        rates of coronary heart disease

5. In recent years, workplaces have adopted exclusionary policies to keep women from hazardous areas. These policies:
   a.   have successfully eliminated hazardous working conditions
        for women
   b.   have protected women and their offspring from hazards
 * c.   have served as a vehicle for sex discrimination
   d.   were forbidden in 1988 by the Pregnancy Discrimination Act

6. Which of the following contributes to a higher accidental
   death rate for men than women?
   a.   reckless driving
   b.   excessive drinking
   c.   differential gender socialization
 * d.   all of the above

7. What is the leading cause of death for young black males
    (age 15- 24)?
    a.   suicide
*   b.   homicide
    c.   cancer
    d.   heart disease

8. With regard to the contraction of Acquired Immune Deficiency
    Syndrome (AIDS), the riskiest form of sexual contact is:
*   a.   anal sex
    b.   oral sex
    c.   vaginal sex
    d.   mutual masturbation

9. AIDS cases tend to be underreported because:
    a.   some physicians are concerned about the stigma attached to
         the disease
    b.   poor record keeping practices in some states and countries
    c.   the long incubation period for the disease makes it
         difficult to determine an accurate infection rate
*   d.   all of the above

10. Women who contract AIDS:
    a.   most likely contract it through blood transfusions
    b.   are disproportionately minority women
    c.   typically contract it through heterosexual sex
    d.   tend to be homosexual
*   e.   only b and c above

11. The illness rate of a given population is:
    a.   the mortality rate
    b.   the life expectancy
*   c.   the morbidity rate
    d.   the contagion rate

12. Women's higher morbidity rates for acute illnesses and
    chronic conditions:
*   a.   are probably related to their longer life expectancy
    b.   are artifacts of physicians' better care of female patients
    c.   are products of their unique hormonal make up
    d.   reflect their greater hypochondria

13. During the 19th and early 20th centuries, wealthy white
    women were especially susceptible to illness. This phenome-
    non:
    a.   can be explained by genetic deficiencies
    b.   was shared by poor and immigrant women also
*   c.   was the result of real symptoms being caused by "styl-
         ishness"
    d.   was unexplainable by medical doctors of the period

14. With regard to the sex distribution of workers in the health care industry:
* a. women constitute the majority of workers
  b. women constitute one half of all physicians
  c. women constitute the majority of obstetricians and gynecologists
  d. women constitute the majority of medical school faculty members

15. In the business of health care:
  a. men outnumber women as a percentage of aides and attendants
  b. nurses' salaries now approximate those of physicians due to the nursing shortage
  c. men are almost 90 percent of the labor force
* d. the least prestigious and lowest paying jobs tend to be filled by minority women
  e. all of the above

16. Recent research comparing male and female physicians' care of female patients shows that:
  a. male physicians are more cautious than female physicians in that they order on average significantly more tests, such as mammograms and pap smears
* b. female physicians tend to care for female patients better than male physicians do
  c. male physicians are favored by female patients
  d. there is no difference between male and female physicians in the care they give to female patients

17. All of the following are goals of the feminist health care movement EXCEPT:
  a. to educate women about health care issues
  b. to open clinics everywhere to help women
* c. to directly challenge the economic organization of society
  d. to influence public policy concerning health care

18. In sport:
  a. women have been encouraged to participate directly in contact games and exercise
* b. serious female competitors are frequently stigmatized as "unfeminine"
  c. women have more opportunities than men since they have special roles, such as cheerleader
  d. women and men can now be considered equal in terms of the amount of money spent on their athletic programs

19. Title IX of the Education Amendments Act:
  a. bars women from competing on men's athletic teams
* b. prohibits sex discrimination in sports
  c. legitimizes the allotment of more federal money to men's sports than women's sports
  d. both a and b above

20. Recent studies of the media's sports coverage indicates that:
    a. women receive only about 50% of televised sports news coverage
    b. women athletes promote a kind of "orthodox masculinity"
  * c. when female athletes are highlighted in the media it is typically as either sex objects or as victims
    d. all of the above

21. The identification of mental illness:
  * a. is often predicated on gender stereotypes
    b. may be affected by a patient's sex, but not her or his race
    c. appears to be based on stereotyped images of femininity, but not masculinity
    d. is unrelated to sex or gender

22. Men who deviate from traditional norms of masculinity:
    a. are rewarded by the mental health care system
  * b. run the risk of being labeled psychologically disturbed
    c. are perceived positively by mental health professionals but not by the general public
    d. rarely elicit a response, either positive or negative, from mental health professionals

23. Mental health professionals:
    a. are more likely to label homosexuals than heterosexuals as healthy
    b. are more likely to diagnose men than women as depressed
    c. are less likely to label women than men as anorectic
  * d. are less likely to diagnose whites than blacks as violent

24. Research indicates that _____ have the highest rates of depression of any group.
    a. minority men
  * b. minority women
    c. white men
    d. white women

25. Married men:
    a. have higher rates of mental illness than never-married men
    b. have higher rates of mental illness than married women
    c. have higher rates of depression than never-married men
    d. have higher rates of depression than married women
  * e. none of the above

26. High rates of depression among minority women are best explained by:
    a. the learned helplessness hypothesis
    b. the matriarchal household hypothesis
  * c. the social status hypothesis
    d. the ritualized aggression hypothesis

27. A person who exhibits a histrionic personality may also exhibit a "conversion reaction" which is:
  a. changing negative behavior to positive in the presence of an authority figure
  b. a fear of open spaces
* c. experiencing illness that has no apparent organic cause
  d. behaving violently toward religious figures

28. The majority of agoraphobics are:
* a. women
  b. members of racial minority groups
  c. over 65 years old
  d. all of the above

29. With respect to alcohol consumption:
* a. men outnumber women among heavy drinkers
  b. men are more likely than women to drink alone or in private
  c. female heavy drinkers are shown more tolerance than male heavy drinkers
  d. employed women tend to engage in more stress-related drinking than non-employed women
  e. all of the above

30. Evidence with respect to illicit drug use shows that:
  a. middle-class youth have increased their recreational use of marijuana
  b. females are more likely to be habitual users than males
  c. male and female patterns of use are now converging
* d. there appear to be no sex differences in terms of pressure to try illicit drugs; both males and females are influenced by male peers

31. Studies indicate that more women than men are addicted to:
  a. heroin
  b. legally prescribed marijuana
* c. tranquilizers
  d. alcohol

32. Research indicates that women who enter drug/alcohol treatment:
* a. receive less support from their families and friends than men who enter treatment
  b. have little difficulty finding programs that will accept them along with their dependent children
  c. are more likely than men to report that they have friends and family who will support them during the treatment process
  d. both b and c above

33. Relative to obese women, obese men:
    a. suffer more negative consequences for being obese
    b. are more stigmatized for deviating from cultural norms of physical attractiveness
  * c. are less likely to lose socioeconomic status as a result of their obesity
    d. all of the above

34. With regard to the physical weight of men and women:
    a. men tend to be more obese than women
    b. poor minority men are the most overweight group
  * c. women tend to overestimate their actual weight
    d. men tend to overestimate their actual weight

35. _____ engage in eating large quantities of food, and then purge themselves by vomiting or using laxatives.
    a. chronic dieters
  * b. bulimics
    c. anorectics
    d. obese people

36. Most anorectics are:
    a. young men
    b. working-class women
    c. middle-aged women
  * d. middle- and upper-class women
    e. members of racial minority groups

37. Women who embrace traditional feminine roles are more likely than non-traditional women to be:
    a. bulimic
    b. agoraphobic
    c. histrionic
  * d. all of the above

38. Sexual abuse of patients by therapists:
    a. is relatively rare
  * b. often induces reactions in the patients similar to those of incest victims
    c. tend to be perpetrated against young males in particular
    d. is most effectively deterred by threats of malpractice suits

39. Feminist therapists:
  * a. try to establish egalitarian relationships with their clients
    b. discourage clients from taking an active role in therapy
    c. focus on clients' interpersonal difficulties to locate the source or cause of their psychological problems
    d. emphasizes individual change rather than institutional reform

True/False:

40. The average woman can expect to live seven years longer than the average man.
   * a.   true
     b.   false

41. Women's mortality rate for respiratory cancer has increased greatly since 1970 due to the fact that more women have taken up smoking.
   * a.   true
     b.   false

42. Women are more likely than men to die from job-related causes.
     a.   true
   * b.   false

43. Available data show that 95% of those afflicted with AIDS are homosexual men.
     a.   true
   * b.   false

44. The number of midwives decreased after 1900 because of their association with witchcraft.
     a.   true
   * b.   false

45. The rate of caesarean births in the U.S. has been deemed medically appropriate by the Centers for Disease Control.
     a.   true
   * b.   false

46. Recent studies show that most physicians do not respond as quickly to female patients' symptoms of heart disease as they do to male patients' symptoms.
   * a.   true
     b.   false

47. The authors of your book argue that some mental disorders are related to cultural stereotypes regarding gender.
   * a.   true
     b.   false

48. Stereotypical feminine behavior is assumed by many clinicians to be the norm of mental health for all women.
   * a.   true
     b.   false

49. About half of American women use psychotropic drugs.
   * a.   true
     b.   false

50. Diagnoses of eating disorders are increasing among minority women and low-income women.
   * a.   true
     b.   false

Essays:

51. Discuss various causes of death that are gender specific. Have there been any changes in recent years as a result of changing gender norms in U.S. society?

52. What is AIDS? Address myths about the disease and methods of prevention.

53. How has women's normal biological functioning been medicalized? Provide specific examples and discuss the consequences of this medicalization.

54. Discuss the traditional doctor-patient relationship and the implications this has for women and men as patients and practitioners.

55. Discuss eating disorders in relation to traditional gender expectations for men and women.

56. Explain how beauty norms in our society are both racially and gender normed. What are the consequences of this norming for those who do not "measure up"?

57. Discuss how the mental health system in the United States has historically rewarded conformity to traditional norms.

58. The U.S. health care system has been called "racist, sexist and class-biased". Based on your understanding of the chapter, argue either for or against this allegation.

Classroom Activity/Take-home Assignment:

This is an exercise on body images. Few of us, especially women, have positive or realistic images of their bodies. Ask each of your students to weigh themselves. They should then record their notion of their ideal weight next to their actual weight. Subsequently, have your students secure a standard weight chart (such as the Metropolitan Life Insurance Company's height and weight tables showing the "Ideal" Weight). For how many students was their actual weight within 10 percent of the official average for their age and height? These students are of normal weight. But how did they judge themselves? How many of them underestimated or overestimated their ideal weights? Were there sex differences in these misjudgments? Use the results of this exercise as the basis for a discussion of gender stereotypes with respect to health and physical fitness.

Film Suggestions:

Among the many films available on AIDS, we recommend:

1. AIDS: No Sad Songs -- examines the effects of the AIDS crisis on patients and their families through two case studies, one of an AIDS patient and the other of a family member of a person with AIDS (30 minutes; also available in the original 61 minute theatrical version; both available from: Filmmakers Library, 124 East 40th Street, New York, NY 10016);

2. Women, HIV and AIDS -- a documentary about the special problems of women, lesbian and straight, in the AIDS epidemic; discusses some of the difficulties women have in insisting on safe sex; covers women from a variety of backgrounds and thereby raises the social and political implications of AIDS (52 minutes; available from: Filmakers Library, 124 East 40th St., New York, NY 10016);

3. Fighting for Our Lives: Women Confronting AIDS -- chronicles the increase in AIDS cases among women and highlights the lack of programs specifically designed to reach the women who are at greatest risk: minority women; shows how women themselves are taking action in their communities to halt the spread of AIDS (29 minutes; available from: Women Make Movies, 462 Broadway, Suite 500, New York, NY 10013); and

4. Silverlake Life: The View from Here -- a video diary that records the relationship of two men who are deeply committed to one another, but who must confront their mortality because of AIDS (120 minutes; available from: The American Documentary, 220 West 19th St., 11th Floor, New York, NY 10011.

Several films consider the physician patient relationship as well as gender issues in health care provision:

5. La Operacion -- an award-winning documentary on the high incidence of sterilization among Puerto Rican women (40 minutes; available from: The Cinema Guild, 1697 Broadway, New York, NY 10019);

6. I Need Your Full Cooperation -- looks at doctors' control of female patients through dramatizations as well as the use of archival footage (28 minutes; available from: Women Make Movies, 462 Broadway, Suite 500, New York, NY 10013);

7. My Doctor, My Lover -- a segment of the "Frontline" series, this video examines the problem of sexual abuse of patients by therapists by focusing on the case of one woman who sued her therapist for sexual abuse (90 minutes; available from PBS Video, 1320 Braddock Place, Alexandria, VA 22314); and

8.   Taking Our Bodies Back: The Women's Health Movement -- an
insightful look at the women's health movement, especially its
emphasis on self-help (33 minutes; available from: Cambridge
Documentary Films, P.O. Box 385, Cambridge, MA 02139).

Also available from Cambridge Documentary Films (P.O. Box 385,
Cambridge, MA 02139):

9.   Hazardous Inheritance -- examines specific workplace dangers
to reproductive health (24 minutes).

Among the films available on gender and sports are:

10. Women in Sports -- a social history of women's sport participation, emphasizing the progress women have made in recent years
and the role of feminism in that progressive change (28 minutes;
available from: Altana Films, 61 Main Street, Southhampton, NY
11968);

11. Women in Sports and Adventure -- shows women in various
sports successfully challenging gender myths and stereotypes (45
minutes; available from: PBS Video, 1320 Braddock Place, Alexandria, VA 22314; and

12. Women of Gold -- eight Asian Pacific lesbian athletes are
featured positively in this brief documentary (30 minutes; available from: Women Make Movies, 462 Broadway, Suite 500, New York,
NY 10013.

Recommended films on mental health issues are:

13. Women and Depression -- a specially adapted edition of the
Phil Donahue Show in which women from a variety of backgrounds
talk about their experience of depression and how they recovered
(28 minutes; available from: Films for the Humanities and Sciences, P.O. Box 2053, Princeton, NJ 08543);

14. The Last to Know -- examines alcoholism among women, emphasizing how traditional gender norms with respect to women's
"proper" behavior prevents alcoholic and cross-addicted women
from receiving needed help (45 minutes; available from: New Day
Films, 853 Broadway, Suite 1210, New York, NY 10003);

15. Advertising Alcohol: Calling the Shots (second edition) -- a
brief look at how the advertising industry creates new alcohol
consumers, especially among the young; based on the research of
Jean Kilbourne (see Still Killing Us Softly, Chapter 6);

16. I Don't Have to Hide -- made by a woman who once had anorexia herself, this film documents not only her struggles with the
eating disorder, but also those of another woman who had bulimia
for nine years (28 minutes; available from: Fanlight Productions,
47 Halifax Street, Boston, MA 02130).

The following are recommended films on body image:

17. Miss....or Myth? -- a documentary on beauty pageants and the images they promote. The film presents the views of both pageant supporters and protesters and focuses on one pageant, the Miss California Beauty Pageant, and on an annual counterpageant, the Myth America Pageant. The film, although dated, will likely spark discussion and debate in the classroom (60 minutes; available from: The Cinema Guild, 1697 Broadway, New York, NY 10019).

18. Positive Images: Portraits of Women with Disabilities -- sexism and racism often make worse discrimination on the basis of disability. This film was designed to portray positive images of diverse women who each has a disability (58 minutes; available from: Women Make Movies, 462 Broadway, Suite 500, New York, NY 10013).

19. Mirror, Mirror -- a brief, but insightful video in which thirteen women of different ages, sizes, and ethnic backgrounds reveal their ambivalence about their bodies (17 minutes; available from: Women Make Movies, 462 Broadway, Suite 500, New York, NY 10013).

20. A Question of Color -- an outstanding documentary about the painful issues of discrimination within the black community regarding skin color, hair texture, and other features; shows how dominant ideals of beauty can have a devastating effect on individuals who do not conform and can create divisions among women of color within their own communities (50 minutes; available from: Women Make Movies, 462 Broadway, Suite 500, New York, NY 10013).

Resources:

1. The National Women's Health Network (1325 G Street, NW, Washington, DC 20005) is the umbrella organization of the women's health movement and is an excellent source of information on gender-related health issues.

2. Information on AIDS, AIDS education, and AIDS services is available from: National AIDS Network, 2033 M Street, NW, Suite 800, Washington, DC 20036; and the National Resource Center on Women and AIDS, 2000 P Street, NW, Suite 508, Washington, DC 20036. Also contact the Sociologists' AIDS Network, c/o Debbie Indyk, 662 Queen Anne Rd., Teaneck, NJ 07666.

3. Lesbian, Gay, and Bisexual People in Medicine (c/o the American Medical Student Association, 1890 Preston White Drive, Reston, VA 22091) was organized with the goal of improving the quality of health care for homosexual patients and has available materials not only on homosexual health issues, but also surveys on admissions, hiring and promotions policies of medical schools

and hospitals. Contact also: The National Lesbian and Gay Health Association, GWUMC, Office of CME, 2300 K St., NW, Washington, DC 20037.

4.   There are numerous excellent sources of information on gender-related mental health issues. Among them are: The American Psychological Association's Women's Program Office, 1200 17th Street, NE, Washington, DC 20036; The Women's Therapy Centre Institute, 80 East 11th Street, New York, NY 10003; the Association of Gay/Lesbian Psychiatrist, c/o David Scasta, MD, 1439 Pineville Rd., New Hope, PA 18938; the Association of Lesbian and Gay Psychologists, c/o Michael D. Siever, 2300 Market St., #102, San Francisco, CA 94114-1521; the American Anorexia and Bulimia Association, 133 Cedar Lane, Teaneck, NJ 07666; and the Alcoholism Center for Women, 1117 S. Alvarado Street, Los Angeles, CA 90006.

CHAPTER THIRTEEN

Multiple Choice:

1. A group organized to promote a particular cause through
    collective action is:
    * a.   a social movement
      b.   a social aggregate
      c.   the status quo
      d.   a social experiment

2. Which of the following conditions must be met in order for a
    social movement to develop?
      a.   individuals must come to see that their problems are shared
            by others like themselves
      b.   people must realize that their problems are individually
            caused and resolve to help improve themselves
      c.   people must attribute the source of their problems to
            structural or institutional conditions
      d.   both a and b above
    * e.   both a and c above

3. The first wave of feminism in the nineteenth century was composed
    primarily of:
      a.   women of all social classes
      b.   working class men and women
    * c.   middle and upper class white women
      d.   all women

4. Abolitionism was an important catalyst for the women's movement
    because:
      a.   it united women in a common cause
      b.   it provided women with a framework to understand their
            inequality
      c.   it allowed women to speak at public conventions for the
            first time
    * d.   both a and b above

5. Women won the Constitutional right to vote the United States
    in:
      a.   1932
    * b.   1920
      c.   1890
      d.   1868

6. The early women's suffrage organizations:
      a.   fought for the enfranchisement of all people
      b.   despised racism and fought heatedly against it
      c.   refuted all stereotypes of feminine behavior with their
            political actions
    * d.   were mainly concerned with winning the vote for women

7.   After the vote was won:
     a.   feminism gained momentum, especially among young women
  * b.   feminism lost most of its active supporters
     c.   feminists were able to recruit more members from the rank of
          "emancipated" middle-class housewives
     d.   feminism disappeared completely until the 1960s

8.   All of the following factors contributed to a resurgence of
     feminism during the early 1960s EXCEPT:
     a.   the publication of Betty Friedan's book, THE FEMININE
          MYSTIQUE
     b.   the report of the Presidential Commission on the Status of
          Women
     c.   women's experiences as participants in the civil rights and
          anti-war movements
  * d.   the Supreme Court's decision in Bowers v. Hardwick

9.   All of the following have been identified as factors that
     contributed to the demise of the Equal Rights Amendment
     EXCEPT:
     a.   amendment supporters underestimated the power of the
          opposition
  * b.   amendment supporters focused too heavily on regional
          attitudes and failed to gauge national trends
     c.   ERA backers often misread national opinion polls
     d.   ERA opponents successfully used scare tactics to per-
          suade many Americans in unratified states to oppose
          the amendment

10   The branch of feminism that seeks to eliminate both capital-
     ism and gender inequality to achieve liberation is:
     a.   the National Organization for Women
     b.   working-class feminists
  * c.   socialist feminists
     d.   liberal feminists

11. Radical feminists can best be described as:
     a.   reform oriented
  * b.   woman-identified women
     c.   working class
     d.   communists

12. Working class feminism has its roots in:
  * a.   women's involvement in trade unionism
     b.   university-based political activism
     c.   the lesbian rights movement
     d.   the anti-Vietnam war movement

13. Minority women:
    * a.   often express stronger support for the women's movement than
           white women
      b.   view the women's movement as the best way to address the
           problems of minority men as well as women
      c.   see the women's movement as a source of unity for women and
           men
      d.   are generally pleased with the way mainstream feminism has
           addressed their concerns

14. Which of the following is NOT an argument of antifeminists
    against feminism?
      a.   biological differences of men and women account for
           different sex roles
      b.   feminism deprives women of the protection they need
      c.   women's natural roles are as wives and mothers
    * d.   women are spiritually and morally stronger than men

15. Research on young, college-age women indicated that:
      a.   their involvement in the feminist movement has declined
           dramatically during the 1990s
    * b.   these women are among those most likely to agree that
           the U.S. continues to need a strong women's movement
      c.   their strategies for change are more conservative than
           those of their feminist elders
      d.   these women have been unmoved by recent events such as
           the continued threat to the availability of safe and
           legal abortions

16. European feminism tends to differ from U.S. feminism in
    that:
      a.   U.S. feminists are more concerned about men's as well as
           women's problems
      b.   European feminists focus primarily on reproductive rights
           issues
    * c.   European feminists have been less concerned about securing
           formal legal rights
      d.   U.S. feminists focus on material conditions, especially
           reconciling women's maternal and employment responsibilities

17. Third World feminism:
      a.   places greater emphasis on securing formal legal rights for
           women than U.S. feminism does
      b.   takes a similar approach to reproductive freedom as U.S.
           feminism does
      c.   sees the position of Third World women as best understood
           using a U.S. or Western feminist model
    * d.   has, by necessity, focused more on issues of daily survival
           than U.S. feminism has

18. The men's movement tends to be:
    a. more racially balanced than the women's movement
    b. more politically active than the women's movement
    c. less dominated by middle-class, college-educated individuals than the women's movement
  * d. none of the above

19. What Brod calls the male-identified branch of the men's movement is best described as:
    a. similar to radical feminism
  * b. tending to blame women for men's problems
    c. analogous to socialist feminism
    d. depending heavily on women assuming nontraditional roles to encourage men to explore alternatives

20. Men's rights groups:
    a. receive strong support from most feminists
    b. encourage men to explore the feminine aspects of their personalities
  * c. appear to be anti-feminist
    d. are viewed by most segments of the men's movement as complementary to feminism

21. For gay men, the major politicizing forces for the development of a liberation movement were:
    a. the writings of the men's movement
  * b. harassment and violence by police and the heterosexual public
    c. men's consciousness-raising groups
    d. the anti-rape segment of the women's movement

22. The lesbian/straight split in the women's movement was primarily caused by:
  * a. resistance among straight feminists about giving lesbians a more visible and vocal presence in the movement
    b. the ideology of lesbian separatists
    c. the refusal of lesbians to participate in anti-violence campaigns
    d. none of the above; there is no lesbian/straight split in the women's movement

True/False

23. The Seneca Falls Convention is important for the women's movement because it was here that women were given the right to vote.
    a. true
  * b. false

24. Most women's suffrage organizations at the turn of the century integrated black women into their membership and activities.
    a. true
  * b. false

25. The second wave of feminism began in the 1960's.
    * a.   true
      b.   false

26. "Feminism" is a homogeneous group of women united in the effort to achieve equality of the sexes.
      a.   true
    * b.   false

27. The majority of women in college today are anti-feminist.
      a.   true
    * b.   false

28. One central focus of European feminists has historically been to secure social benefits for families.
    * a.   true
      b.   false

29. The unifying component of all the factions of the men's movement is the support of gay rights.
      a.   true
    * b.   false

Essays:

30. Discuss the history of the Women's Movement. How has it changed from 1900 to the present? What are the interests of the various factions of feminism today?

31. How does Third World feminism compare with U.S. and Western European feminisms? What are the unique contributions of Third World feminism to our understanding of gender inequality?

33. Feminists are often critical of many aspects of the men's movement. Explain these criticisms and discuss why feminists might be skeptical of the men's movement's commitment to ending gender inequality.

34. What are the contributions of the gay and lesbian rights movement to an analysis of sexual politics?

35. The Women's Movement has been accused of being racist, class-biased, and heterosexist. Defend or refute this accusation, citing specific examples to support your argument.

Classroom Activities/Take-home Assignments:

1.   Ask students to reflect on the material they have read in the preceding twelve chapters. It should be obvious to them at this point that gender relations are very different today than

125

they were one hundred, fifty, even twenty-five years ago. Yet, at the same time, they will hopefully recognize that much remains unchanged. Ask them to discuss what they consider to be the three most important changes in gender relations during the second half of the twentieth century. What specific factors and/or people were responsible for bringing about these changes? Then ask them what they see as the three most important aspects of gender relations that still need changing. What strategies do they think would be most effective in securing these changes? This is a good exercise for helping students to begin to consider their role in bringing about social change.

2.   This manual as well as the text itself include information on groups and organizations that are working to address specific forms of gender inequality. Ask your students to select a particular problem of interest to them and then identify a group or organization that is working to address the problem. (The resources we have identified may be utilized, but there are numerous others that students can locate on their own.) Ask each student to report on the history of the group or organization selected, its structure and membership, the specific activities and projects in which it is involved, and where it may be contacted for more information. The class can then combine these reports into a resource guide that can be distributed to all class members or, if funding is available, can be made available to the college or university community.

Film Suggestions:

1.   Women's Rights in the U.S.: An Informal History -- uses a variety of cinematic techniques to trace the history of the women's movement and changes in attitudes about gender; an entertaining social history (27 minutes; available from: Altana Films, 61 Main Street, Southampton, NY 11968).

2.   Daughters of De Beauvoir -- interviews with some of the leaders of the second wave of feminism, including Kate Millet and Ann Oakley (55 minutes; available from: Filmakers Library, 124 East 40th St., New York, NY 10016).

3.   Women in the Third World -- examines the living conditions of women in Third World countries, especially their economic circumstances, and highlights their efforts to bring about change in their societies (30 minutes; available from: PBS Video, 1320 Braddock Place, Alexandria, VA 22314.

4.   A Man's Woman -- an interesting docu-drama about the ideological and social implications of the anti-feminist movement while posing a number of important questions about feminism that women's movement supporters should consider (52 minutes; available from: The Cinema Guild, 1697 Broadway, New York, NY 10019).

5.   Honored by the Moon -- documents the activism of gay and lesbian Native Americans; examines the issue of homophobia within

Native American communities, while Native American gays and
lesbians discuss their unique historical and spiritual roles in
their communities (15 minutes; available from Women Make Movies,
462 Broadway, Suite 500, New York, NY 10013).

Two videos about a particular segment of the men's movement are
available from PBS Video (1320 Braddock Place, Alexandria, VA
22314):

6.   Robert Bly: A Gathering of Men -- an interview of Bly which
also shows scenes from one of Bly's weekend workshops for men,
whom he encourages to develop a deeper understanding of their
grief (90 minutes); and

7.   Save the Males: An Endangered Species -- follows three men
as they explore "male rituals" and attempt to answer questions
such as whether men can reconnect to their male identities
through the freedom and spontaneity of participation in "wildman
weekends"?

Resources:

1.   Women's Action Alliance (370 Lexington Avenue, New York, NY
10017) is an umbrella organization for women's groups and organizations which provides information and referrals as well as
publications on women's programs. An excellent source of information on particular women's groups since it has available group
profiles.

2.   National Institute for Women of Color (1400 20th Street, NW,
Suite 104, Washington, DC 20036) is an outstanding resource for
information and data on minority women and groups for minority
women in feminism; publishes the quarterly, "Brown Papers."

3.   For information on Third World feminism, contact the Third
World Women's Project, Institute for Policy Studies, 1601 Connecticut Avenue, NW, Washington, DC 20009; and the Resource Clearinghouse of the MATCH International Centre, 1102-200 Elgin St.,
Ottawa, Ontario, Canada K2P 1L5.

4.   Perhaps the best resource for men's movement information is
the National Organization of Men Against Sexism (NOMAS), 798
Pennsylvania Ave., Box 5, Pittsburgh, PA 15221, which also publishes an excellent newsletter.

5.   The National Gay and Lesbian Task Force (1517 U Street, NW,
Washington, DC 20009) is an excellent source of information on
gay and lesbian rights activism throughout the United States.
Contact also: the National Center for Lesbian Rights, 1663 Mission St., Suite 550, San Francisco, CA 94103.

Other resources worth noting are:

6.   The Women's Hall of Fame, located in Seneca Falls, NY, in

the same church where Alice Paul launched the ERA campaign in
1923. Kept at the hall is memorabilia of the first wave of
feminism as well as materials honoring hall of fame inductees,
such as Shirley Chisholm; and

7.   Two email forums of interest are:

      a. H-WOMEN: for scholars and teachers of women's history;
to subscribe:

      Send the message: SUBSCRIBE H-WOMEN <YOUR NAME> (again,
your real name, not your email id)

      to: LISTSERV@UICVM (bitnet) or: LISTSERV@UICVM.UIC.EDU
(internet); leave the subject line blank.

      b. PROFEMEN: a profeminist men's forum; to subscribe:

      Send the message: SUBSCRIBE PROFEMEN <YOUR NAME>

      to: LISTSERV@DAWN.HAMPSHIRE.EDU (internet); leave the
subject line blank.

NOTES

NOTES

NOTES

NOTES

NOTES

NOTES